SUICIDE

SUICIDE

The Will to Live
vs.
The Will to Die

Edited by **Norman Linzer**

Professor, Wurzweiler School of Social Work
Yeshiva University, New York

HUMAN SCIENCES PRESS, INC.
72 FIFTH AVENUE
NEW YORK, N.Y. 10011

Copyright © 1984 by Human Sciences Press, Inc.
72 Fifth Avenue, New York, New York 10011

Printed in the United States of America
123456789

Library of Congress Cataloging in Publication Data

Interdisciplinary Educational Conference on Bereavement and Grief
(7th : 1981 : New York, N.Y.)
Suicide: the will to live vs. the will to die.

"Proceedings of the Seventh Annual Interdisciplinary Educational Conference on Bereavement and Grief co-sponsored by Yeshiva University, the Jewish Funeral Directors of America, Inc. and Allied Professions, April 14, 1981."
Bibliography: p.
Includes index.
1. Suicide—Congresses. I. Linzer, Norman. II. Yeshiva University. III. Jewish Funeral Directors of America. IV. Title.
RC569.I55   1981   362.1'96858445   83-18578
ISBN 0–89885–156–4
ISBN 0–89885–190–4 (pbk.)

Dedicated to the Memory of
Dr. Samuel Belkin, President
Yeshiva University
and
George Goodstein, Counsel
Jewish Funeral Directors of America

CONTENTS

CONTRIBUTORS

MORTON BERGER, Ph.D.
> University Dean of Behavioral and Social Sciences and Dean, Ferkauf Graduate School, Yeshiva University.

IRIS BOLTON, M.A.
> Director, Link Counseling Center, Atlanta, Georgia.

RUSSETT PUSIN FELDMAN, M.D.
> Clinical Instructor and Clinical Assistant, Mt. Sinai Hospital, Department of Psychiatry, New York.

RICHARD FOX, M.D.
> Assistant Professor of Psychiatry of New York Hospital-Cornell Medical Center, Westchester Division; Vice President of the International Association of Suicide Prevention and Crisis Intervention.

RABBI JACOB GOLDBERG, M.A., M.S.
> Spiritual Leader, Ft. Tryon Jewish Center, New York; Director, Commission of Pastoral Bereavement Counseling, New York Board of Rabbis.

RABBI EARL A. GROLLMAN, M.H.L., D.D
> Spiritual Leader, Beth El Temple Center, Belmont, Massachusetts; Bereavement Team Member, Harvard University Community School of Psychiatry.

ARIE KIEV, M.D.
Director, Social Psychiatry Research Institute, New York; Author of *Riding Through the Downers*, and *The Courage to Live*.

SAMUEL C. KLAGSBRUN, M.D.
Medical Director, Four Winds Hospital, Katonah, New York; Associate Professor, Jewish Theological Seminary, in Pastoral Psychiatry.

ANN S. KLIMAN, M.A.
Director, Situational Crisis Service, Center for Preventive Psychiatry, White Plains, New York.

WILLIAM S. LISS-LEVINSON, PH.D.
Director, the Brooklyn Hospice, Metropolitan Jewish Geriatric Center, Brooklyn, New York; Chairman, Pain Management Review Committee, Metropolitan Jewish Geriatric Center.

RABBI ISRAEL MOWSHOWITZ, PH.D.
Spiritual Leader, Hillcrest Jewish Center, New York; Past President, New York Board of Rabbis; President of the World Conference on Religion and Peace.

CYNTHIA R. PFEFFER, M.D.
Assistant Professor of Psychiatry, Cornell University Medical College; Chief, Child In-Patient Unit, New York Hospital-Cornell Medical College, Westchester Division.

JOSEPH RICHMAN, PH.D.
Chief, Geriatric Psychology, Jacobi Hospital, New York; Associate Professor, Albert Einstein College of Medicine, New York.

SYDEL SILVERMAN, PH.D.
Executive Officer, PH.D. Program in Anthropology, City University of New York; Professor of Anthropology, Queens College, New York.

JANE SLAVIN-SIMDORN, M.S.W.
Private Practice of Psychotherapy, New York.

ANDREA DIANE SMALL, R.N., M.S.N.
  Clinical Psychiatric Instructor, School of Nursing, Holy Name Hospital, Teaneck, New Jersey.
ARTHUR M. SMALL, M.D.
  Clinical Associate Professor of Psychiatry, New York University School of Medicine; Director, St. Agatha's Home of the New York Foundling Hospital, Nanuet, New York.
RITA REIS WIECZOREK, R.N., P.N.P., ED.D.
  Associate Professor of Nursing, Hunter College-Bellevue School of Nursing, New York.

FOREWORD

Yeshiva University has held all-day conferences on bereavement and grief since 1974. The 7th Annual Interdisciplinary Conference on Bereavement and Grief, co-sponsored by Yeshiva University and the Jewish Funeral Directors of America, Inc., and Allied Professions was held on Tuesday, April 14, 1981, at Yeshiva University's Brookdale Center at 55 Fifth Avenue in New York. The theme of the conference was, *Suicide: The Will to Live vs. the Will to Die.*

In the general area of bereavement and grief the theme of suicide is considered particularly crucial, given the enormous increase of attempted and actual suicides and the complex problems with which professionals of various disciplines are called upon to deal.

The conference objective was to help professionals understand the phenomenon of suicide and be able to deal with its complexities as they provide service to individuals who contemplate and attempt suicide, as well as to bereaved survivors.

This was an all-day conference. The morning was comprised of a keynote address, *Psychotherapeutic Approaches to the Suicidal Patient,* by Ari Kiev, M.D., followed by two presentations, *The Significant Others and Their Role in Suicide Prevention,* by Jane Slavin-Simdorn, M.S.W., and *The*

Samaritans: An Alternate Approach to Suicide Prevention, by Richard Fox, M.D.

The afternoon was devoted to fourteen workshops. Eight dealt with detection, prevention, and intervention with potential suicides, with separate workshops on children, adolescents, youth, and terminally ill, and the special role of the pastoral counselor. Four workshops dealt with intervention with bereaved survivors of suicide. Two workshops, dealing with special aspects of suicide, discussed cultural attitudes in relation to suicide and "slow dying" as a form of suicide.

The final portion of the day, the plenary session, included an address by Rabbi Earl Grollman, *First-Line Help (Clergy and Funeral Director) Following a Suicide* and a closing address, *The Status of Approaches to Suicide Prevention in Today's World.*

Close to 600 people attended this conference, attesting to the concern regarding the whole question of suicide. It was a most rewarding and enriching experience to coordinate this conference. I am greatly indebted to all the participants, and to Deborah Miller, my associate coordinator, in particular, without whose dedicated involvement the conference could not have been as successful.

Frieda M. Pusin, M.S.W.
Faculty
Wurzweiler School of Social Work,
Yeshiva University
Conference Coordinator

PREFACE

In recent years there has been a rising rate of suicide among all age groups, and a spate of books studying the phenomenon. Suicide is a major mental health problem in the United States, as it is in most of the civilized nations of the world. It raises not only legal, ethical, philosophical, and moral problems, but also professional concerns, namely detection and prevention. The mental health practitioner faced with a suicidal patient confronts an enormous task and burden—preventing the fatal act. It is an awesome responsibility that requires keen perceptive ability, special knowledge, and great sensitivity to the individual who threatens suicide. This book, the proceedings of a conference on suicide, is designed to help practitioners acquire more knowledge and become more aware of the issues involved in suicide motivation, prevention, and treatment.

The time is ripe for another book on this subject because of social factors and the particular features of this volume. Literature abounds on death and dying. Courses on the subject have proliferated on college campuses, and departments of thanatology have been established. Cultural events such as TV shows and plays have dramatized the need to be more open and sensitive to the dying and to bereaved families, and to engage in the subject with less fear and denial. The 600 participants at the Bereavement and Grief Conference have joined this cultural trend, as have the authors who shared their knowledge, research, and experiences with them.

There are special features that, when combined into one volume, make this book unique among others on the subject. First, the presentations encompass the "before" and "after" of suicide. The primary emphasis is on detection, prevention, and intervention; but when these fail, practitioners must become involved in the family's bereavement process in order to help them deal with the special grief emerging from suicide.

Second, several chapters treat particular issues of prevention among specific age groups, namely children, adolescents, youth, and adults and aged who are terminally ill. The depression of each age group that may lead to suicide takes different forms and has a distinct etiology, of which mental health practitioners need to be informed.

Third, the roles of a variety of mental health practitioners are delineated. The psychiatrist is most prominent, but the roles of the therapist who is a social worker or a psychologist, and of the nurse as part of the health care team are amply described. Among professional roles, that of the pastoral counselor is described in different perspectives by three rabbis representing the clergy. It reflects Yeshiva University's conviction, as an educational institution under Jewish auspices, that religion can help people deal with the stresses of status passage.

Fourth, the chapters combine both descriptive and prescriptive propositions concerning suicide. The phenomenon is analyzed from many angles, and research studies are cited to describe causes, factors, and intervention strategies. Prescriptively, principles of intervention are then introduced to guide the practitioner in the treatment process. The methods suggested are direct and professionally sound.

Fifth, the material is illustrated by cases culled from the author's professional experience. These have the effect of supporting the theoretical perspective, and they "humanize" the discussion. One entire chapter contains a mother's vivid account of her son's suicide and the aftermath of pain, grief, healing, and growth.

Several common themes permeate the book. Depression as a major factor leading to suicide is discussed by many of the authors. As anger and rage turned inward, depression is a leading indicator of suicide potential. For treatment approaches, there is widespread consensus that the patient must be individualized, that suicidal tendencies represent a real crisis in the person's life not to be treated lightly, that the therapist needs to stay with the patient for as long as it takes to control the impulse, and the family can serve as the most important source of emotional support for the patient. The family is the symbol of significant others—social structures that may include friends, relatives, and benevolent strangers manning a suicide hotline.

We believe that this volume will make a contribution to the professional literature on suicide because it deepens the understanding of its nature, and offers various therapeutic approaches toward its prevention, and toward the bereavement process after a suicide has occurred.

The Bereavement and Grief Conference and these proceedings were made possible through the joint efforts of the Jewish Funeral Directors of America and Yeshiva University. Under the dynamic motivating force of Andrew Fier, Burton L. Hirsch, Herbert Kaufman, Sonny Levitt, Stanley Robinson, Joseph Roth, and Richard Stein of the funeral directors, and the inspired leadership of Dr. Herbert Dobrinsky of Yeshiva University, the conference has become an annual educational event that has attracted thousands of participants over the years to its varied themes on death and dying. Frieda Pusin, the conference coordinator, did a valiant job in carrying out her mandate and following through on collecting the papers from the presenters. We are deeply indebted to Norma Fox and her skilled staff of the Human Sciences Press for their confidence in the educational and professional value of this book.

Norman Linzer

Part I

DETECTION, PREVENTION, AND INTERVENTION WITH POTENTIAL SUICIDES

A. General
B. Life Cycle

A. General

INTRODUCTION

Section I, which deals with the "before" of suicide, is divided into two parts: general and life cycle. General aspects of suicide detection, prevention, and intervention encompass its causal factors, and social groupings and professionals who can be mobilized in prevention efforts. The life cycle focuses on understanding the motivations for suicide by various age groups, the impact on family members, and the differential roles of mental health professionals.

Chapter 1, *Suicide and Depression,* prevents an overview of one of the major causes of suicide. Depression is generally not recognized as a factor in suicide because mood swings are part of normal human experience. Yet it is the most important variable among others, such as the attitudes of significant others, the individual's cultural values, and the impact of stress experiences on everyday functioning. The therapist must use different approaches for patients with depressive illnesses, character disorders, and the socially isolated. The therapist is urged to persist in his or her efforts, even if home visits are required, and to treat the family along with the patient.

Chapter 2, *Significant Others and Their Role in Prevention* stresses the important function of family and friends in preventing suicide. There is a need to involve these significant others in the treatment process from the onset. The treatment team might consist of a therapist for the patient and a therapist for the family. This structure is necessary because the suicidal person's needs are sometimes more than one therapist can handle. The therapists meet with the family to present their evaluation of the situation and how the family should proceed. Through a case presentation the author substantiates her claim for the involvement of significant others—the family in particular—in the treatment process because they provide support and emotional nurturance that act as a buffer against the urge to die.

Chapter 3, *The Samaritans*, logically follows the previous chapter in the emphasis on social supports as critical factors in suicide prevention. Here the social group consists of significant others who are *not* known to the suicidal person prior to contact. The Good Samaritans is a group of volunteers in Great Britian who operate a hotline for potential suicides. They are guided by these principles: the service is available 24 hours a day, a drop-in center is available for individuals to speak to counselors directly who will lend support and friendship, and anonymity is protected. The Good Samaritans is not part of any coercive system and encourages the caller to be in charge of his/her own destiny. The author suggests the adoption of the idea in other countries as a significant social support system for suicide prevention.

Chapter 4, *Intervention with Potential Suicides,* follows the previous discussions with an emphasis on the role of the therapist as a primary preventer. After discussing the phenomenon of the cultic suicide of Jonestown in the light of various theories of suicide, the author cites the increase of suicide in our society as a public health problem of major proportions. After a brief review of therapeutic approaches, the author presents case illustrations from his own practice which suggest that the therapist must take an exceedingly directive and authoritative role so as to harness the patient's dependency needs, while at the same time carefully avoid provoking the patient's hostility by appearing aggressive. The therapist must project an image that is at once soothing and omnipotent in the ability to remove the source of the unbearable panic, thus obviating the patient's need to escape into the suicidal alternative.

Chapter 5, *The Special Role of the Pastoral Counselor with Potential Suicides,* adds another professional role to that of therapists in suicide prevention. The pastoral counselor is among the first whom the potential suicide calls for help. The clergyperson occupies a significant place in the helping structure as a representative of the religious institution. Fundamentally, suicide is a religious problem; it signifies the loss of meaning in one's life, the loss of self-definition and purpose. Signals for the potentiality of suicide include depression, loneliness, loss of a loved one, change of status and fortune, continuous anger turned inward, and severe illness. The clergyperson has the responsibility to help the individual to regain a sense of meaningful living by invoking theological principles regarding the dignity and worth of every human being, the divine concern for each individual, the possibility for change and repentance, and belonging to a religious fellowship. He/she listens intently to the individual, universalizes feelings of unworthiness, invokes the family's strength and concern, and introduces the idea that life is a precious gift to be cherished.

Chapter I

SUICIDE AND DEPRESSION

Ari Kiev

The incidence of suicide in the U.S. is approximately 11 per 100,000 people; that is, between 25,000 and 30,000 are listed every year as dead from suicide. But the actual number has been estimated to be twice that. The rates have remained relatively the same since the turn of the century, except for the Depression, when the rates went up, and World War II, when the rates went down. In the past 20 years, the rates of suicide have tripled for young men of fifteen to twenty-five and doubled for young women of fifteen to twenty-five, while among the elderly, the rates have diminished somewhat.

Within this framework, three demographic variables are consistently associated with increased risk. The risk of suicide increases in every age group progressively with increasing age except among women where it seems to level off in the sixties.

In our culture, sex is another critical risk factor. Men

kill themselves three times more often than women do. Although women attempt suicides as often as men, the methods they have used, until recently, have been less lethal and generally reversible. They have used pills, gas, or self-inflicted lacerations rather than jumping from high places, hanging, or firearms.

Marital status is another critical factor which seems to protect individuals. The incidence of suicide is greatest among the widowed, single, or divorced, and lowest among those who are married.

These major demographic variables—age, sex, and marital status—consistently show significant relationships to suicide rates. While religious, cultural, and socioeconomic factors no doubt have some relationship, they tend not to be as consistent. Moreover, the published figures are not broken down in terms of these variables.

Additional risk factors which have been identified in various studies include a past history of abuse of alcohol and narcotics, a family history of suicide, rejection of the sick role, and a nonsupportive and punitive attitude of significant others toward a patient with psychiatric illness.

Constant vigilance and awareness of some of these more subtle factors is of great importance since some 50 or 60 percent of those who kill themselves are in some kind of treatment at the time. In fact, 80 percent of those who kill themselves have made some effort to get help or to communicate the fact that they were feeling suicidal within the previous 6 months. The suicidal crisis occurs so rapidly that patients slip through the treatment net or are not followed up.

One reason for this is the failure to recognize depression as an illness. To the extent that we all feel down from time to time and that mood swings are part of normal human experience, there is a tendency to think that depression can be alleviated by diversion, a pep talk, or change of activity.

Another reason for the high incidence of suicide among patients in treatment is that we're dealing with something we can't predict. Suicidal behavior results from a combination of events: depressive illness, attitude of others, and whether an attempt has been made in the past which makes it easier for them to repeat the event. These multivariate factors have to be operating simultaneously to increase the chances that the individual is going to attempt suicide.

Whether or not a patient complains about symptoms of depression and even persistent thoughts of suicide has great prognostic significance. In our own studies of high-risk patients who had made one or more suicide attempts, we found that the patients who expressed distress about their symptoms had a more favorable prognosis than those who kept quiet about them, seemed resigned, and did not want to burden others with their problems. The absence of expressions of distress would seem to be associated with higher risk for a subsequent attempt either because patients have given in to their fate or receive insufficient attention because they are silent about their problems.

A related finding was the fact that patients in conflict with others—a common phenomenon among these patients—had a better prognosis than those who experienced minimal or no interpersonal conflict. In effect, the worst prognosis was to be found among patients who somehow didn't make enough noise or cause enough trouble. Those were the people who, while in treatment, in hospital, or discharged and followed as outpatients, kept their feelings to themselves and didn't communicate distress to other people or get others concerned about them, and thus tended to set in motion a cycle of neglect. Often they began to feel that nobody really cared.

This group of low-profile, uncomplaining patients included those who might have made suicide attempts that were judged to be gestures or of minimal suicidal risk. The severity of the attempt was not as critical a variable in determining subsequent outcome as was the degree of discomfort and distress reported by patients. Frequently patients are admitted to hospital as emergencies, treated and rapidly discharged. They feel better after being pumped out or sewn up, and are judged to be improved. They are sent home without provisions being made for follow-up treatments, when in fact they may still be at significant risk, especially immediately after hospitalization and at least for 1 year thereafter, or until the factors leading to the attempt have changed.

By contrast, some patients accidentally take the wrong pills and come close to dying or have to be put on the artificial kidney and hospitalized for several days. As a result of the fact that they came close to dying, they are likely to be judged as more disturbed psychiatrically and be hospitalized for an extended period of time.

There is a definite tendency to provide the most intensive care to patients who are the most medically ill rather than to patients who are the most psychiatrically ill, or, more important, the people for whom other significant factors such as the degree of distress, difficult life situations and relationships with others, and other stressful life experiences suggesting that they are likely to be high-risk patients.

One of the critical variables to consider in evaluating patients, perhaps more important than how the patients attempted suicide or what they are planning to do, would be the attitude of the people who have an impact on them.

In our studies we did all kinds of factor and cluster analyses. The most significant variable proved to be the attitude towards the patient of the significant others in the patient's life: husband, wife, parent, friend, neighbor. Whoever it was, if there was a punitive, moralizing attitude—an inclination to say, "Snap out of it, there's no reason to lie in bed all morning feeling sorry for yourself or not eating—(generally, an attitude which patients themselves frequently had) coupled with depressive symptomatology, there seemed to be an increased risk of suicidal behavior.

Efforts to encourage patients to "snap out" of their depression intensify feelings of guilt, inadequacy, and hopelessness and may stimulate suicidal preoccupations. This is particularly so because such promptings imply that the depression and nonfunctioning are motivated rather than symptomatic of an underlying psychobiological process. If patients already have a critical, puritanical view of their nonfunctioning, they will only be made to feel worse by this additional pressure.

A supportive, paternalistic approach to the patient wherein the family is encouraged to view the depression as an illness in need of specialized treatment, encourages the patient to enter the "sick role" and assume some of the patient's responsibilities, and is a far more helpful approach. In the later stages of treatment strategies for reducing stress can be introduced to the patient.

The therapist may be dealing with a lot of people talking about suicide but must figure out which ones are likely to have the highest risk. To look only at the patient, you may miss the event that will occur. You have to look at the environment the patient is living in: the support systems and the attitudes of the supportive people.

If you look at the suicide rate around the world, this point of view is confirmed. In South America there is a kind of "mañana" attitude and the suicide rate tends to be very low. In Scandinavia where there is a strong sense of the "Protestant work ethic," and the need to achieve, you'll find a much higher rate. The point is that the culture and attitude transmitted through the families are important in determining whether an individual with a depressive illness will ride out the depression and accept the symptomatology as evidence of the illness which requires bed rest, a reduction in responsibility, and a relinquishing of burdens, until such time as the illness passes. Even without treatment, most such illnesses will eventually remit. Even if the individual does nothing, recovery is very likely. The problem is the eagerness or anxiety of other people to try to do something to force the patient to improve, or for the patient to force him or herself to improve, and that invariably leads to the greater risk.

What I've tried to emphasize is the presence of denial. People deny there's an illness to be treated or that has to run its own course. An emphasis is placed on utopian notions that jogging or eating certain diet foods or doing yoga will have an impact on the basic underlying condition.

There is considerable evidence in the biological and neurophysiological work now going on at the National Institute of Health and elsewhere that fundamentally we are dealing with a stress-related phenomenon which has a biological basis. The usual kinds of things we do to make ourselves feel better will not have an effect on a real depression. What one needs is time, a reduction of stress, or major antidepressant medications which increasingly are becoming more specific for particular conditions. In fact it is now possible to differentiate one type of depression from another on the basis of symptomatology and the basis of biochemical and physiological assays.

It might prove useful to see how we differentiate among the different kinds of patient groupings that one is likely to see in a suicide prevention clinic or other setting where one is dealing with high-risk groups. I have divided these into three groups: patients with depressive illnesses, patients with character disorders, and a group of socially isolated individuals who show progressive deterioration over time.

Decisions about treatment should be based on an assessment of this whole array of variables including the patient's psychopathology, past history of suicidal behavior, and willingness to enter into the sick role; relationship with others and the attitudes of others towards the patient's problems. One of the critical issues in dealing with patients is their entry into the sick role. This is why a lot of suicides occur when the patient is in transition.

We have recently looked at some of our own data and experiences. Because we specialize in treating suicidal patients, therapists frequently refer patients who are beginning to become suicidal. The patient has become depressed and has begun to talk about suicide or is going into acute panic. At one time, we thought because we were experts that we would take these patients on. Now our approach is to encourage the patient and therapist to maintain their relationship.

We might take the patient on and provide antidepressant medication and see him/her in conjunction with the therapist. At the time of transfer, the suicide rate seemed to rise. The therapist says he or she can't handle it and refers the patient to experts who believe they can. After the first visit, you never see that patient again because the patient goes home and kills himself or herself. This is not because the second expert has failed, but because the patient feels rejected or has not established a link with the therapist. He or she feels abandoned. The primary therapist just does not know how to deal with the situation because such patients are often very demanding, sullen, and so depressed that nothing works. They can really wear a therapist out. It's at that point, where the therapist has had a long day, is tired, has personal problems, and forgets that over a period of time he or she has been providing a tremendous amount of support to this person, even though the results can't be seen or the individual is always complaining. So the therapist says, "Well, I think you're right; I can't help." Such therapists think they are doing the right thing by referring the patient elsewhere. To some extent it may be helpful to give the therapist a new perspective by learning what has been going wrong or what else he or she can do. But it is not helpful completely to discharge the patient.

We have realized in the past few years that it is really important not to give up. When the therapist gives up, it may turn out that the patient has been testing the therapist. The patient may be discouraged. But as long as the therapist isn't discouraged, and continues to bear with the patient, you keep the risk of suicide down.

I've seen patients referred for evaluation. Just that fact alone suggests that the therapist couldn't handle it anymore and pulled the rug out from underneath the patient. It is really critical, in that transition zone, to maintain the contact. Beyond that, there are patients who are simply unwilling to get into treatment. It's hard to treat somebody who is not in treatment. The moment the individual agrees to get into treatment, he or she is, to a small extent, protected. It doesn't matter how psychotic or how suicidal the patient's preoccupation, as long as the person is willing to enter into treatment, no matter what form it is, you have some kind of control over the suicidal behavior.

It's not that acting out is suicidal as it is really a sense of discouragement or a sense of having been abandoned, and a sense of futility which increases the patient's risk of suicide.

Sometimes the same phenomenon occurs in the patient's home setting. We saw a man this year, a policeman in his sixties, who had numerous hospitalizations and suicide attempts. He seemed to respond to medicine, but as he began to feel better, he had a certain amount of conflict at home with his wife—she was still anxious about the possibility that he might kill himself, even though he was improved—and she and her daughter would spend hours pursuing him, following him around just to watch him. This created a tremendous amount of anxiety in the patient. When the family talked alone, they seemed to suggest that because of their great anxiety, they would feel relieved if he finally went ahead and killed himself. One must be aware of the point when the family can't stand the strain anymore.

The wife discouraged him from continuing treatment; he was hospitalized, and came back again. Shortly thereafter, he was reluctant to make any more appointments because he didn't think he was getting anywhere and didn't know what to do at home or how to spend his time. The wife was agitated, and reluctant to get into treatment. The man hanged himself.

The point I'm making is that significant others sometimes reach a point where they, too, feel so frustrated because of their own pathology, their own intolerance, that they begin to communicate this to the patient. The patient, in turn, feels like a burden to the family, and believes they'd be better off without him or her. That attitude at home is a difficult one to modify.

It's easy to treat the patient who wants help and the family who is glad he's getting help and is supportive of him. The suicidal patient is the one who ultimately slips out because the family is discouraged, the patient doesn't want to make the trip in, and the dynamics in the home situation are such that the patient feels the family would be better off without him or her.

Perhaps it is a failure on the part of the therapy team to take a very vigorous crisis intervention approach. In retrospect, if we had made home visits and emphasized the fact that this man needs to be in treatment, and went out of our way, maybe we might have prevented the policeman's suicide. But it's that special effort which sometimes one doesn't realize is necessary until it is too late. Going the extra mile is often critical in managing such patients.

Patients with character disorders often appear healthier than they are. This leads the attending physician or the relative to conclude that the suicide was motivated by the wish to elicit sympathy or attention or both. Frequently a husband will be hostile towards his wife or the wife feel neglected and drink excessively, thereby accentuating a cycle of punitive, critical judgments on the part of the husband towards the patient. Or there are instances where a youngster is becoming increasingly suicidal and self-destructive and even violent, and the family keeps reinforcing this behavior by tolerating or condoning it. They complain they don't know what to do or how to handle it. It is only when it is confronted as a family situation—that the whole family has to come into treatment—that they see it is the family relationship which needs to be treated.

Frequently it is not until the situation gets out of hand that the family is willing to confront this and face up to it. They realize they have to set limits and change their behavior at home. Environmental factors must be considered. The family has to be brought in and all the factors that may have triggered the suicide crisis have to be incorporated in the treatment process. All people involved should be encouraged to enter into treatment. The patient may minimize problems while the significant others tend to be indifferent, rejecting, punitive, or overcontrolling in their concern for the patient's welfare.

The family of the suicidal patient very often plays a significant role in the development and perpetuation of the suicidal crisis. Especially if the family is punitive, hostile, and controlling, it is essential to involve them in the therapeutic process so as to reduce their noxious impact on the patient and change the relationship. Without involving the family, the risks remain very high.

This is particularly true with socially isolated individuals who show progressive deterioration of function over time, periodic psychiatric symptomatology, a basic alienation from others, and who have no apparent support systems in their life. Such patients generally have a lifelong history of severe psychopathology and multiple life stresses, particularly in terms of family and social isolation. They frequently attempt suicide at a distance from others, make no effort whatsoever to be rescued, and require special efforts to keep them in treatment.

When you get such patients in treatment, the first objective is to reduce self-perpetuating and self-cycling strategies which intensify and perpetuate the problem. The second objective is to ensure that the patient remain in treatment and can be followed over an extended length of time. Once having established this framework, appropriate psychotherapeutic and psychopharmaceutical methods can be employed more effectively.

Once the patient has passed the initial crisis and symptoms have been relieved by effective use of antidepressant medications and the family is involved in the treatment process, and once the patient has learned some basic strategies, he or she can begin to focus more concretely on individual psychopathology. It may be a question of learning responsibility or learning to be more assertive. With some high-achieving, perfectionist people who are incapable of saying "I need help" or "I need support," it may be a question of learning to ask for help. Some patients are often more comfortable in the helping role. In fact it's incredible how often patients who have tried suicide have told me that they regularly have three or four friends who constantly consult them for advice. Such people often feel responsible for taking on the burdens of the world or their friends and have a lot of people leaning on them while they themselves haven't learned how to ask for help.

In the later phases of psychotherapy, emphasis should be placed on trying to help the patient and perhaps the family develop greater awareness about unconscious behavior patterns and interpersonal interactions which may be increasing stress and causing problems for the patient. The basic task is to help the patient overcome dependency, understand the relationship of past experience to the present, and overcome and deal with obstacles in the achievement of personal objectives. Here, the greatest emphasis is placed on autonomy and self-reliance in order to reduce some of the vicious cycles of dependence, resentment, guilt and self-deprecation which exist. Masochistic efforts to fail and suffer often derive from unrealistic needs to meet the expectations of others and/or from fear of seeking one's own objectives.

Chapter 2

SIGNIFICANT OTHERS AND THEIR ROLE IN SUICIDE PREVENTION

Jane Slavin-Simdorn

It is very difficult to approach this subject without an awareness of the pitfalls of suicide prevention.

Everyone who works closely with suicidal patients and significant others know that we have not discovered a method which will prevent all suicides. As much as we have researched the subject and understand the phenomenon, the overall rate of suicide has not significantly changed. Families and individuals are daily being devastated by the tragedy of self-destruction. We, therefore, as clinicians, must approach each case of suicidal crisis with a set of guidelines that we know, through experience, will maximize our chances of reversing the destructive possibility, aware that there are no guarantees.

The theoretical guidelines and model of intervention to be discussed have evolved over many years of working with the families of attempters and suicides. Significant others are an integral part of maintaining the suicidal person's connection with life. Their help is needed for supporting the person during the crisis. Their presence, patience, understanding, and tolerance provide the therapist with a much needed leverage against the urges of the suicidal "to give up," "escape," or "free others from the burden of their problems." In order to fulfill this role significant others need guidance, understanding, and support. Their plight must be addressed with the same urgency and empathy as is given the suicidal person. They are, in fact, facing their own crisis and the level of stress they frequently have endured must be a simultaneous focus of therapeutic intervention in suicidal cases.

Much has been written in suicide-prevention literature about the responsibility of significant others to be the first line of prevention. They are the ones who are supposed to recognize the potential of suicide and take action. They are expected to perceive the import of subtle clues of a waning investment in living and the implications of suicidal ideation and behavior in depression. Further, they are expected to encourage the troubled friend or relative to seek professional help, or when that fails, to seek help on their behalf.

Surely many attempts and suicides would be averted if significant others were able to meet these expectations in the early stages of a developing crisis. The fact is that in most cases they are not. Not only do they face very real obstacles in perceiving the need for help, but when they do, they are frustrated in their efforts because of the structure of mental health services and the persistence of the notion that therapy only helps the self-motivated. This paradox comes about because of the very basic human responses to a possibility of a major loss or threat to security. This seriously limits the capacity of spouse, parent, etc. to act before the problem reaches crisis proportions. It also accounts for much of the behavior that has been identified as noxious and in fact a contributory factor in the etiology of suicide.

Early signs of emotional distress will not signal significant others to an urgent situation. Usually they attempt to explain the behavior in terms of a simpler problem and one that is manageable through a series of steps that have worked for them or someone else in the past. When the problems are not solved but worsen, and a member of the family begins to act or talk directly about suicide, significant others respond not unlike those suffering from anticipatory grief. As denial is no longer possible they can become angry, resentful, and begin to blame the suicidal family member for not trying to help him or herself or criticizing the professional help the relative may be receiving for not bringing about a resolution of the problem. It is not uncommon for relatives to become overprotective and excessively controlling. As their anxiety increases they may make more demands on the suicidal person to pull him or herself together or to act out their rage in response to threats with statements that indicate indifference. Given that the significant others may witness an actual attempt they may take a defensive posture of beginning the process of emotional detachment. All of this negatively affects the suicidal person, reinforcing a belief that the problems are unsolvable. This very charged volatile situation is what confronts a therapist in most high-risk suicidal cases.

Since the primary goal of intervention is to reverse the process which is leading to suicide, it is imperative to involve significant others in the treatment process from the onset. What I am suggesting is, in every case where suicide is a possibility, significant others should be involved in treatment. The most practical way from a psychological point of view of carrying this out is with the establishment of a treatment team: a therapist for the suicidal patient and one for the family.

If a therapist works individually with such cases the demands from all those involved will be overwhelming. The suicidal person's needs are sometimes more than one therapist can manage. Trying simultaneously to deal with the demands from significant others can only seriously dilute the effectiveness of therapy.

Therefore, two or even three therapists can collaborate in providing service. Although this works best in group practices or clinics, a private practitioner can use it through the establishment of a temporary working relationship with a colleague who has experience in family therapy or crisis intervention.

The requirement of the involvement of the significant others is spelled out at the referral stage, and when made a simple stipulation for the initial appointment, it is rarely a problem. The initial assessment of significant others' reaction and the defenses employed to meet the crisis are a valuable part of the assessment, evaluation, and choice of treatment for the suicidal patient. This is particularly important in determining whether to accept the situation on an outpatient basis or to recommend hospitalization until the emotional climate of the home can be altered.

The family's therapist defines his or her role as that of an ally of theirs, identifying and expressing understanding of the myriad reactions they are having. The fact that this is a serious situation is emphasized and the lack of complete guarantee of success is clearly explained.

One of the first areas of focus is the fact that responsibility for and control of the outcome lie ultimately in the hands of the suicidal person. The magic sought by significant others has to be faced and a realistic approach to the problem worked out.

Treatment goals of the individual's therapist are conveyed to them and what is needed of them is also explained. When the situation is sufficiently calmed down to warrant it, a family meeting is arranged and conjointly the therapists present their evaluation of the situation and recommendations for management. Periodically these meetings will take place to bring about needed changes in the family's interaction and to promote the positive attachments.

Therapy with the family focuses on educating them about suicide and the warning signs of expected setbacks. They often must be taught to listen. It is very difficult to be told about a problem without voicing ideas or coming up with alternative solutions. Yet often people in distress want and need just that.

For example, family members, on hearing about a problem, offer various explanations of possible causes or feel they must give advice on how to solve it. When their advice and/or suggestions are not acted upon, they begin to lose patience and express frustration or tedium about repetition of the problem. Also, they can get caught up in specifics of the complaints and not realize that it represents a general sense of despair, or as in one case we saw, represents a reaction to the loss of purpose or function.

Case Illustration

This case involved a sixty-eight year-old man, his wife, and adult daughter. The man had retired about a year before from the fire department. He had been successful, achieving recognition, and enjoyed the challenge and camaraderie of his job. Not long after retirement, when leisure and gardening lost its appeal, he developed a series of physical complaints. The family was concerned particularly about severe stomach pains and his fear that they were an indication of cancer. After being supportive through

diagnostic testing and brief hospitalizations, they were relieved to learn that there was nothing seriously wrong with
him. His complaints persisted, and with them his family's
patience diminished. He then began a series of psychotherapy sessions and a trial of psychotropic drugs. He
would initially feel better, and then the pains would recur.
Finally, in the context of continued physical and mental
distress, he overdosed on his medication, was hospitalized,
and released not long after as somewhat improved.

The family had not been seen for more than some
history-taking, and were given information that his problems had no physical basis. The situation continued to
plague the patient and his family. Finally a second attempt
was made, this time involving the wife's having to cut him
down from hanging. The patient was left with no memory
of the incident, and after about a week of hospitalization
was considered not actually suicidal and not committable.

The process of blame, fear, and resentment was well
entrenched when we were asked to see the patient and the
family. The wife was no longer able to provide support.
She was tired of hearing about his stomach pains and was
excessively anxious about future destructive behavior. The
adult daughter was caught in the same ambivalence of
wanting to help and resenting the situation. Family intervention was initiated. Unfortunately, by this time a destructive pattern was set. The family and the patient were looking for miracles and did not continue contact. Efforts to
reinvolve them failed, and the man killed himself after developing another physical symptom and completing
another series of diagnostic tests and doctor-shopping.

Early intervention may have prevented his death. It
certainly reinforced for us the importance of the family
needing guidance and adequate information about the suicidal member's problems, as well as being helped to cope
with the interpersonal effects of depression.

It also reinforced our knowledge of the role most often assigned to the significant other—that of reporter and historian. Rarely is suicide treated as a family problem, and yet it is the most potentially devastating threat to family life we know.

Another common focus is the pattern of dependency which occurs quite frequently in families where one member is suicidally depressed. Frequently it is the member that the family has come to rely on and continues to burden even while recognizing that they cannot meet these demands. Strengthening the other's capacity to tolerate tension and more self-reliance often takes a great deal of time but is beneficial to all concerned.

Conclusion

There are many corrective steps that have to be taken by the suicidal person and the family if suicide is to be avoided. This model represents one of the ways of achieving that goal. It relieves therapists, the suicidal, and the family from the overwhelming demands of the crisis.

The significant others' role in prevention is an important one. They provide the support, emotional nurturance, and attachment that act as a buffer against urges to die. Without help, they cannot maintain this function.

Chapter 3

THE SAMARITANS: AN ALTERNATE APPROACH TO SUICIDE PREVENTION

Richard Fox

A very strange thing has happened with regard to suicide during the last 20 years in Britain. In England and Wales, which is by far the principal statistical and administrative unit, suicide rates have been remarkably stable and predictable since they were first recorded 120 years ago—about 10–11 per 100,000, very much as in the USA. Suicides were less, as always seems to be the case in wartime, from 1914–18. The rate reached an all-time low, for that time, of 9 per 100,000 in 1941 with the Nazi forces at our gates, and little more than a few ancient rifles loaned from the USA to repel them. On the other hand, at the height of our Depression, in 1931, the rate peaked at 15. The decline after the U.S. peak in 1936 was coincident with the relief measures for the poor and unemployed.

After World War II, suicide rates in Britain climbed predictably back to their "normal" level, the rise being steeper for women than men, as in all Western countries, and parallel to the changing pattern of other sorts of illnesses, such as lung cancer and heart disease. "As ye live, so shall ye perish." The nationwide introduction of electroshock therapy (ECT) during the years immediately after the war, which most believed to be the most rapid and predictable way of relieving that kind of severe depression that leads to suicide, made no noticeable dent in the upward trend. Again, although invaluable in the treatment of many severely depressed people, the introduction of tricyclic antidepressants, far from having had any discernible effect on suicide statistics, seems to be taking the place of barbiturates for use in attempted suicide overdose.

After the postwar peak in 1963 when the rate was just over 12 per 100,000, there was a remarkable and consistent annual decline to an all-time low of 7.5 in 1975—that is, a drop of 40 percent or some 2,000 people every year out of a population of 45 million who decided, against all the odds, to go on living after all. The strange thing, of course, was that the odds at this time were stacked heavily in favor of a suicide rise, with increasing unemployment, unstable governments, devalued currency, and progressive industrial anarchy. And, one might add, no war to come to our rescue! No statistician, however compulsive and hypercritical, has doubted the truth of this decline. The law against suicide was repealed, but that made no difference, and suicide as a taboo cause of death became more, rather than less, acceptable with the spread of humanistic doctrines alongside other statistically deviant, and formerly taboo conduct, such as abortion, homophilia, and other paraphilias. You will have heard of the organization *Exit* which encourages suicide under certain circumstances and has compiled an instruction booklet.

A comparable decline has happened in no other country, the general rule being, as in the USA, a steady rise; so, what happened?

Much ink has been spilled among students of suicide arguing about it. Was it a switch from lethal town gas (around 13 percent carbon monoxide) to safer North Sea gas and imported methane? The figure looked good, but when Holland, and more recently France, "department" by "department," made this transition, there was no change in the steady upward rise of suicide. Professor Erwin Stengel noted as long ago as 1965 that when the town of Basel detoxified its gas, people drowned themselves instead. Removing a method of suicide does not work, as any Durkheimian would expect. Suicide is the outcome of an interplay of complex socioeconomic-politico-theologico-psychologico-medico factors, and probably lots of other things as well, of which we have so far scant comprehension.

The World Health Organization did sponsor a study of intervening variables throughout European countries to try to account for changes. The results were underwhelming; the closest things to correlate with suicide rates were the number of television licenses and children born to women under twenty. And there were exceptions to those. To suggest that British doctors are better at recognizing and treating suicidal depression than the Scandinavians or Swiss is just insulting; and intensive care of overdosers, reduced use of lethal barbiturates, greater use of virtually nonlethal benzodiazepines, better care for the elderly, welfare support for the underprivileged and unemployed, are done better in countries other than in Britain.

There is, however, one unquestionable intervening variable between Britain and other countries, and that is a curious volunteer organization called Samaritans. Samaritans started out in 1953 from central London when a clergyman used an advertised phone number directed at people in distress. As the first "hotline," it got massive publicity and callers flowed in. Helpers, thank God, flowed in too, and the name "Samaritans," which was given by an amiable journalist, somehow stuck. Though arising within the Anglican (Episcopal) Church, Samaritans has been, from the first, totally nondenominational, nonevangelistic, nonpolitical. Though we would have quite liked to change the name to something with no religious connotations, like "Befrienders International" which is the name of Samaritans worldwide, it was too late. We were stuck with a name of wide applicability and addressed to the distressed, despairing, and suicidal from whatever cause, much like such special service lines as Marriage Crisis, Youth Lines, Drug Lines, Gay Lines, etc.

Through the 1950s, the organization and the principles of the movement were laid down, and they have remained virtually unchanged. The cornerstone has been the immediate, *24 hour availability* by hotline in relation to anything the caller wants to talk about. Not being a specific suicide service has the advantage that many who might be in terrible trouble, but who didn't seem themselves at that time as suicidal, might ring before it was too late. Studies of those who survived desperate suicide bids show how ambivalence exists right until the fatal act—those who grab at balconies having jumped from high buildings.

The second principle was the *drop-in center,* open daylight hours or later, where people could come with or without appointment to talk to someone who was "just another human being" without being preached at, counseled, or therapeutized. Or, one might add, charged any kind of fee! Emergency outreach teams, on rota call, termed "Flying Squads," go out in exceptional crisis circumstances.

The third principle was *one-on-one befriending,* whereby these ordinary human beings, the helpers, offered friendship in a systematic way to other human beings who were in a jam, mostly to the lonely and the bereaved, where the helper stood in for the absent friend or relative, and helped the distressed person re-establish links with life. Arising from this was that any such fellowship cut clean across any kind of race, class, or creed barriers, recognizing only the value of the individual human being, whoever, or whatever, he or she may be. Being unshockable and non-judgmental was very much a part of this, which could make it hard for a strict Roman Catholic helper, say, to befriend a girl whose overriding wish was for an abortion; but it is done.

Other vital principles have been the principle of *anonymity*, in which the caller is at liberty to reveal his or her identity, reveal a pseudoidentity, or just remain anonymous, without anyone pressing for name, address, next of kin, and social security number. These are required introductions to most, if not all, professional helping agencies and seem to be a significant barrier for a great many callers in need. It flows from this that the caller is at all times in charge of his or her own destiny. Helpers are not professionals and don't pretend to be experts. Indeed, the strength of Samaritans may life in its *not* being part of any coercive system, including psychiatric committals and law enforcement. The 1 percent or so who come having committed a crime, so they say, are mostly persuaded to make it right with their consciences and with society and give themselves up. They are usually accompanied to the police station by their befriender and by one of the many hundreds of attorneys who give their services free to the Samaritan movement. Violent hands are not laid on the remainder, nor on those who say, after talking things out, that they are going to go and commit suicide, just the same. The usual experience, again, is that they return after second thoughts asking to talk some more.

It is my belief that for many suicidal people, the harder one tries by *coercion* to prevent their suicide, the more one raises their resistances, to make that suicide more likely. Dr. Kiev referred to the role of significant others. Whether that relationship be with clergyman, physician, friend, relative, bartender, funeral director, or Samaritan, this is the best way to keep people alive. There are particularly high rates of suicide among those who have been bereaved by suicidal death. Special programs have been designed to direct prevention efforts towards this group.

Helpers have to be recruited, of course, and to a degree selected, so that those with specific vulnerabilities do not damage themselves or the callers. They have to be prepared for what they are likely to meet. The word "preparation" is preferred to "training" in that one cannot be trained to be a warm human being. Preparation classes normally comprise 7 separate evenings and role play has increasingly taken the place of formal instruction. I am talking about "caller" instead of "client" or "patient," as these have clinical connotations which are outside this movement. I prefer to talk about "helper" rather than "volunteer" because this latter term seems to have been denigrated of late under the partial influence of the women's movement.

There are about as many male Samaritan helpers as there are female, certainly among the young and the retired, though I have to confess a certain preponderance of middle-aged women whose children have become independent and who find a new kind of fulfillment through Samaritan work. Indeed, housewives form the largest single group among our Center directors. In this country, where directors of this type of helping agency are expected to have a Ph.D. at the very least, this may come as a surprise. We professionals have a part to play in receiving referrals of those who need specialized treatment, so that a better title to this presentation might have been "The Samaritans, a *Complementary* Approach to Suicide Prevention," rather than an *Alternate* one. Samaritan centers are expected to have a consultant in both family medicine and psychiatry, to take part in preparation, trouble-shoot with their colleagues, and be around if the director wants help. However, central to Samaritans is the volunteer thrust. They are the people who run the service, whether you want to call them volunteers, helpers, or, to coin a happy phrase, "ordinary people." They also make the service strikingly cost-effective, the average all-in budget in Britain being about $10,000, or one-third of what one would pay a professionally trained center director over here. It comes out to about $4 a caller! To make it work, there has to be a fairly complex leadership network among experienced helpers with specific leaders assigned to such tasks as recruitment, supporting helpers, organizing the roster, being on duty to deal with crises, representation on other organizations, etc. In one small country branch where the callers were fairly few, no less than 80 percent of the helpers were involved in some kind of administrative task, down to the person who made sure there were pencils and paper in the duty room. There is a message for us, in all of this, in these times of funding cutbacks.

These essentials being established, Samaritans mushroomed through the 1960s, the maximum growth spurt coinciding with the suicide decline. Saturation has just about been reached with 175 centers serving all towns of over 60,000 population, with an average of 120 helpers per center, or 21,000 in the British Isles. As a U.S./U.K. comparison, Greater Los Angeles with the largest urban sprawl in the world has *one* Suicide Prevention Center (which by the way sees itself as a research rather than service organization). Greater London has 14 centers. Samaritans are known to almost every adult Britain, the public image is extraordinarily positive, and information about the essentials of confidentiality, etc. is surprisingly accurate. Skeptical Americans have stood on the high street of some town asking casual passersby the way to the Samaritan Center and have very seldom been met with a blank stare. About a quarter of a million people make calls to Samaritans every year in Britian. It is reasonable to assume it to be a high-risk population as 40 percent have been shown to contact Samaritans while harboring active suicidal thoughts—very many times the random incidence of such thoughts. The Medical Research Counsel in England showed that callers who lapsed from contact had a very high suicide rate during the following year—equivalent to that of herion addicts. An equivalent organization in the USA would expect 5 million calls.

This remarkable organization has implications for suicide prevention far beyond the actual work done. Many patients of mine who never made contact felt reassured just by the fact that the organization was there and carried the phone number of the nearest center in their wallet. With an approximate turnover of 20 percent of the volunteers every year, something over 100,000 people have been released, as it were, into the community with a knowledge of Samaritan principles and the importance of caring. They could be "leaven" in engendering caring attitudes, amid the daily concourse of the nation.

I end, appropriately, with a commercial. *New York NEEDS Samaritans. The New York Post* on February 28, 1980 carried a headline, *Suicide Hotline Tells Woman to Drop Dead.* Other than this center in Queens there is Dr. Vincent Peale's "Help Line" operating by phone only from a secret place and referring any suicidal caller to the National Save a Life League which seems, again, to act essentially as a referral agency on as near to a 24-hour basis as their 30 or so volunteers allow. Again, the premises are kept secret, calls may be put on "trace" and distressed persons may find themselves, very much against their will, collected by the police and taken via some emergency room to Ward's Island. If this information were to filter around the suicide-prone communities in psychiatric units it would not be the best way to attract distressed people to call their friendly suicide prevention service.

Something is very much needed. Aspects of guilt and shame have become built into the three religions mainly represented in New York. Islam and Christianity have taken their concepts of mortal sinfulness from Talmudic origins. Haim Cohn, speaking at the International Suicide Prevention meeting in Jerusalem in 1976, offered the exceptions to mortal sinfulness such as the Masada type situation of inevitable torture and conduct contrary to the Laws. He offered a new interpretation arising out of the Hebrew term for suicide, "He who destroys himself knowingly." If this cannot be proved by two eye-witnesses, there may be an assumption of pathological depression or mental disturbance such that the suicide is considered nonvoluntary, the result of "insane minds," and therefore excusable. The equation of suicide with insanity, of course, is dangerous and does little to dilute the essential shamefulness of suicide, for which perhaps the Jewish and Roman Catholic communities punish themselves the most. Cases treated with great sensitivity are obviously less likely to have come my way.

The medical examiner in Cork, for example, known as one of the most traditional parts of southern Ireland, is said never to have recorded a verdict of suicide in his career. I could describe cases without number where families, physicians, and clergy entered a benign conspiracy to conceal the truth. This shame, and the fears attendant on talking to suicide patients, may make patients reluctant to talk to their therapists about what is literally a life-and-death issue and may make the therapists, again collusively "not want to hear" for reasons such as fears of their therapeutic impotence, for their reputation, and of malpractice suits.

Few therapists feel comfortable when a patient expresses suicidal thoughts, and, paradoxically, the psychiatrist may be the last to know of the patient's suicidal intent. Here are problems of countertransference indeed! This collusive silence can embrace whole institutions, for example, universities, from which it has been virtually impossible in Britain to obtain data on suicides or suicide attempts among students.

Yet for a suicidal person to reveal this deep, dark secret can be as cathartic as the proverbial lancing of an abscess. To do so anonymously, to someone who is "outside the family" as it were, and to be accepted in loving and nonjudgmental fashion, may make this positively life-preserving. Guilt can kill, but *shame* can kill equally.

In New York there is a nucleus of people who see the need for the Samaritans of New York City, which include increasing numbers of experienced helpers from the five Samaritan Centers in the USA, of which Boston's is the largest and oldest (founded in 1974). Although no one has *proved* that Samaritans were associated with the suicide decline in Britain, the relationship is persuasive. Anything to increase the amount of circulating friendship and caring can be no bad thing. Professor Allardt, the Finnish sociologist who was advisor to the United Nations, studied everything he could about the Scandinavian countries to find out why Norway had half the suicide rate of the other four. One significant constellation emerged: social cohesiveness, family cohesiveness, and general friendliness. In Norway people were friendlier to each other.

Conclusion

We have seen how individual psychology tends to pass to interpersonal psychology, and the importance to the distressed person of his or her position in the social matrix. This was particularly well expressed in the earliest known writing on suicide, a man's dialogue with his soul which was written on papyrus around 2,000 B.C. and is in the Berlin Museum:

Death is in my sight today
Like a well trodden way,
As when a man returns home from an expedition.
Death is in my sight today
Like the clearing of the sky,
Like a man attracted thereby to what he knows not.
Death in in my sight today
Like the longing of a man to see home,

Preceding these moving words is the following:

To whom shall I speak today?
Faces are averted,
Every man has (his) face downcast towards his
brethren.
To whom shall I speak today?
Hearts are rapacious,
No man has a heart upon which one can rely,
To whom shall I speak today?
There are no righteous men.
The land is left over to workers of iniquity. . . .
To whom shall I speak today?
I am laden with misery
Through lack of an intimate.

Chapter 4

INTERVENTION WITH POTENTIAL SUICIDES

Morton Berger

This is an unusual week to be speaking about suicide. There can be no discussion of the topic which does not come to grips with the enormity of the events that took place just a little over a week ago. The names Jonestown and People's Temple are burned into the minds of all of us who have presumed to deal professionally with the problem of suicide, as are the words of the eyewitness whose account was published in the lead article of the *New York Post* on November 21, 1978.

> Mothers held their squirming infants as a cult doctor and two nurses spooned or squirted some of the cyanide-laced grape Kool-Aid into their mouths.
> Some mothers of older children gave them paper cups filled with the lethal concoction before drinking it themselves.

Several others injected the poison directly into their veins as armed guards circled the open-air pavillion.

Arm-in-arm, family members whispered of the "dignity of death" and waited to die. It took about five minutes.

Then convulsions and last gasps for air distorted their smiles into grisly masks. Their eyes rolled upward and they fell dead—many still arm to arm.

Being brought into direct confrontation with the act of suicide is for most of us a gut-wrenching experience, though many of us become inured to it as we read about the instances in our daily papers. An event like Jonestown, however, because of its scope, is likely to bring these suppressed feelings back to the surface. That was its effect upon me. It evoked a childhood memory that was repressed for some 35 years. I was about eight years old when, while walking along Columbus Avenue in Manhattan, I had my first direct encounter with the phenomenon of suicide. The victim was a woman in her early sixties named Mrs. Tompkins whom I had known casually since she and her husband ran the local candy store. She had obviously jumped from the window of her apartment some four or five stories above the candy store just moments before my arrival on the scene. I vividly recall my emotions at the time which were essentially a feeling of fear, but much more a profound sense of perplexity. At the time I was wrestling almost every night with the feelings engendered by the recognition of the inevitability of my own death, and could not understand why anyone would willingly give up that most precious possession which ultimately will forcibly be taken from all of us. The events at Jonestown aroused in me the very same sense of profound perplexity.

Most of us who are engaged in the scientific study of

human behavior learn early to accept humbly a scientific principle known as the doctrine of emergence. This says that as we form theories designed to summarize and perhaps explain the information that we have gathered in regard to a particular phenomenon and deductively derive hypotheses from these theories, we may test to generate the evidence to confirm or disconfirm all or part of the theoretical formulation. We must ever be aware of the fact that at any moment information or data may appear on the scene that is "emergent" with respect to existing theoretical formulations. This is to say, our existing theories simply cannot serve to explain the data. At that point we must begin to think about revising our views. The events in Guyana represent an example of emergence with respect to the existing views which attempt to explain suicidal behavior. The phenomenon of mass group suicide is certainly unheard of in our experience. To those of us who have an even passing acquaintanceship with Jewish history, it evokes a memory of events that took place some 2,000 years ago on the fortress of Masada, though the psychological similarity between the two events is, in my view, a superficial one.

This chapter will review several ideas which have been expressed by eminent writers in the field which have been particularly useful in dealing with suicidal behavior. These ideas will be examined in light of the emergent data generated by the phenomenon of Jonestown and some insights will be derived with regard to the relative significance of some of them. Some of these ideas will be examined in light of my own experience in working with suicidal patients.

Perhaps the most important idea regarding the approach to the study of suicidal behavior was expressed by psychiatrist Lawrence S. Kubie (Schneidman, 1969):

I shudder whenever I hear a sentence that begins, "Suicide is . . . " We know that there is such a thing as
people ending their own lives and there is such an
event as suicide which can be studied, but "suicide" is
an abstraction made from generalizations about many
extraordinarily subtly different processes—even
though the end result has a unique constancy with
uniquely consistent consequences. This last fact de-
ludes us into thinking that all these are one phenomenon.

He points out that there is a commonly held fallacy
that all suicidal behavior is motivated by a desire for self-destruction. In fact, the exact opposite is very often the case.
Many writers in the field have emphasized that the underlying psychological process in most suicidal individuals is
one of intense ambivalence, the internal conflict between
the desire to live and the desire to die. At any given point
in time one or another of the drives gains ascendancy and
we tend to think that that is the dominant motivational
mode of the individual. We must always be aware of the
fact that the individual who was suicidal a month ago, a
week ago, a day ago, may not be suicidal at the moment
and may again be suicidal in a day, a week, etc. In this
connection, Farberow (Shneidman, 1967) suggests that the
suicidal individual is at that time in the state of crisis and
must be seen thus.

There is a *zeitgeist* in our country at this time which
tends to ignore the crisis aspect as well as the underlying
ambivalence and the complex nature of this behavior. This
zeitgeist has its roots in the democratic tradition of individual
liberty and the recently elaborated ego psychology which
emphasizes individual choice, self-enhancement and self
actualization. The slogan of our time is "do your own
thing." When this is carried to its logical extreme it may

lead to self-destructive behavior. We speak of victimless crime when the only victim is the self. If the right of self-determination is carried to the logical extreme, the concept of intervention in the suicidal crisis is called into question in that it is an interference with the individual's right of self-determination.

This has an interesting parallel in the Jonestown event where the lines between behavior that is motivated by a free intelligent choice, behavior that is the result of external coercion, and psychological manipulation (by means of behavior-modification techniques and environmental manipulation), are blurred. The accounts of the Jonestown suicide indicate that there were elements of coercion and yet many people did appear to be exercising free choice. It is also known that behavior modification techniques were used to overcome the natural disinclination of individuals to end their own lives and those of their children. One can argue that every suicidal act is overdetermined in this way, and that the line between rational choice and pathological compulsion will most often be blurred (though in some cases, such as suicide in schizophrenics and psychotic depressives, the weight of evidence appears to be pretty clear). The decision in regard to intervention is therefore basically a philosophical one.

From my point of view, the decision is a simple one. In the case of suicide, the irreversibility of the outcome and the devastating effect on significant others require that we err in the direction of presuming pathology, and intervene. Farberow (1967) claims that we must intervene actively in order to deal effectively with the suicidal crisis. Therapy must be characterized by activity, authority, and involvement of others. This activist approach can be justified as a response to what Shneidman and Farberow (1961) call "the cry for help."

Karl Menninger (Shneidman, 1969) says,

I think it is important to distinguish suicide as a form
of death and suicide as an attempted expression of
something within one; helplessness, desperation, fear,
and the other emotions. In the past few years I have
tried to say that all symptoms that we recognize in
psychiatry, all the things we have considered in the
past to be evidences of illness except those directly
dependent upon brain lesions and poisons, are all de-
vices that are actually sacrifices offered to avert suicide
and the dreadful decision that there is nowhere else
to go.

Kubie (Shneidman, 1969) says, "to assume that every
act of self-injury has self-extinction as its goal is a serious
fallacy. Sometimes, the conscious and unconscious goals
may be precisely the reverse."

In my experience I have had occasion to interview, in
depth, a number of individuals who made serious suicide
attempts which were thwarted by chance. The attempts involved such methods as taking poison, hanging, and lethal
overdose of medication. My impression in all of these cases
was that at the moment of crisis, the ambivalence generated
so much anxiety that the suicidal act or the decision immediately preceding it had a very reinforcing anxiety-re-
duction effect. In all the cases the ambivalence returned
some time later on, and in most instances was resolved in
favor of the desire to live. In retrospect, all of those people
clearly welcomed the intervention although they freely admitted that at the time it was most unwelcome. The anxiety-
reduction hypothesis may very well serve to explain the
seemingly docile behavior of the masses at Jonestown, once
they came to believe that the decision was made and there
were no alternatives. In my view, therefore, the decision
must always be in favor of intervention.

Suicide in Society

The nature of the larger problem also demands intervention. As Dublin (Shneidman, 1967) points out, there are over 25,000 suicides in the United States each year. The best estimate is that there are seven or eight attempts for each completed case, that is, from 175,000–200,000 attempts in the United States each year. He goes on to say, "Nor are these attempts to be dismissed lightly; they are all cries for help: many, very desperate appeals. Because they involve young people for the most part, their numbers accumulate over the years. I estimate that today there are not less than two million persons alive in the United States who have a history of one or more such attempts."

When one considers the numbers involved, one quickly realizes that this is a public health problem of major proportions. Furthermore, there are good reasons to believe that in the absence of comprehensive strategies for intervention the problem will very likely get worse and the total numbers will increase. There are several reasons for this. We know that there are seven to eight attempts for each completed suicide. If the nonintervention approach were to prevail, then the likelihood decreases that the problems giving rise to the attempt would be addressed and possibly ameliorated. It is also known that someone who has attempted suicide in the past is far more likely to attempt it and to succeed in the future than someone who has not.

Furthermore, the external social stresses that have a significant role in generating suicide attempts appear to be increasing. This is particularly true in the case of college students and young adults. Robert Havighurst (Shneidman, 1969), discussing the role of the educational establishment in relation to suicide, quotes a British anthropologist who takes the British educational establishment to task for fostering extreme competitiveness that has resulted in an increase in student suicide. While Havighurst feels that this kind of view represents an exaggeration, he recognizes the problem and cites statistics to the effect that one-third of college student deaths are due to suicide. If we consider the fact that in the past decade there has been a sharp increase in competitiveness and a decrease in opportunity for college-trained students, there is good reason to anticipate that the suicide problems will become even greater with this population.

The faddist aspect of suicidal behavior is a problem that will become more serious. Havighurst cites an incident in Japan in 1933 in which a young woman committed suicide by throwing herself into a volcano crater. The newspapers played up that event and in the succeeding 10 months 143 people committed suicide in the same way. In the year after that, 167 more jumped into that same crater. This suggests an almost contagious aspect to suicidal behavior. The example of Jonestown is, of course, another case in point. One may hypothesize that the example of the group serves to detract from the natural inhibitions on the part of an individual to do something which is generally seen as an exceedingly negative act. At the opposite extreme, the fad can even serve to romanticize what would have otherwise been unacceptable behavior. Here again we see a parallel in the events in Guyana.

Jonestown is telling us that the current fad in which ever-increasing numbers of individuals are joining quasi-religious cults can possibly lead to an increase in suicide. The key psychological element in affiliating with the cult is the abdication of self-determination in favor of submission to peer pressure and cult leadership. The cult demands more than simply obedience. It continually and openly demands extreme forms of behavior whose only rationale is

a demonstration of a commitment to respond almost instinctively to the will of the cult. The mechanisms evident
here are those of Pavlovian and Skinnerian conditioning.
Like the fad itself, this type of manipulation can be used
to detract from the normal inhibitions that people have in
regard to suicidal behavior.

Intervention

The general characteristics of intervention in suicide
cases that Farberow has stressed have already been listed.
We must now focus on the obvious conclusion that the multiplicity of psychological causes will require a variety of intervention strategies. Kubie (1967) lists eight psychodynamic formulations, each of which would require a different therapeutic approach. In the Menninger approach,
suicidal behavior represents the failure of a pathological
defense, and therefore virtually every severe emotional disturbance can be considered a step towards suicide. In such
a system the task of predicting suicidal behavior becomes
almost impossible.

Shneidman, Farberow, et al. (1961) have presented an
approach that consists of combining leading dynamic factors underlying suicidal behavior with personal information that relates to the statistical likelihood of successful
suicide attempts. This not only provides a basis for predicting the likelihood of suicide but also yields some strategies
for coping with it, as well as a series of priorities in directing
our efforts.

Litman and Farberow (1961) list information that
should be obtained in order to assess the self-destructive
potentiality of a particular individual. This includes factual
information such as age and sex, onset of self-destructive
behavior, methods of possible self-injury, recent loss of

loved person, medical symptom, and emotional resources available to the individual. They also include such factors as status of communication with patient, kinds of feelings expressed, reactions of referring person, personality status, and diagnostic impression.

These categories were significant in some of the more salient statistical findings of Shneidman and Farberow (1961) in their study of suicides in Los Angeles. They found that while more females than males threatened and attempted suicide, more males than females committed suicide. They also found that the older the individual the greater the likelihood, particularly for males, that the threat would be carried out. Litman and Farberow (1961) state, "we have rarely encountered a nonlethally intended suicidal action in a man over fifty." On the other hand, young females between fifteen and thirty-five provide the largest number of self-destructive, nonlethal communications and suicidal attempts. Very often, manipulation is the primary motive for this group.

One of the major danger signals of lethality is a history of recent personality changes combined with a history of recent suicidal attempts. In such acute situations immediate intervention on a crisis basis is necessary. Long term outlook for changing this pattern is favorable. If, on the other hand, there has been a long-term pattern of repetitive self-destructive behavior, the eventual outlook becomes quite pessimistic. While emergency intervention may be necessary, it usually has no lasting effect. The individual's fantasies regarding the suicidal act are most important, and its degree of specificity and realism is a key in assessing the seriousness of the immediate problem. The additional symptoms are the recent loss of a loved person and medical problems. The following two cases from my own professional experience illustrate some of these points.

Case Illustrations

I had been seeing a twenty-three year-old woman in individual psychotherapy for approximately a year. She had a history of hospitalizations for an acute psychotic episode and was diagnosed as suffering from schizophrenia. At the time I was seeing her, she showed no active signs of psychosis; however, she was depressed, led a rather solitary existence, showed sleep and appetite disturbance, and consistently made statements reflecting hopelessness and worthlessness. She spoke of suicide often, and expressed extreme hostility toward her parents whom she blamed for her emotional problems. One day she called me to announce that she had just ingested a month's supply of tranquilizing medication, but would not tell me where she was. It was clear that this was a manipulative device, and her call to me was, at the same time, a plea for help and a means of punishing me for not satisfying her dependency needs sufficiently.

In direct contrast to this case is that of a twenty-four year-old man with whom I worked for about a year in an art therapy group conducted for in-patients at a V.A. Hospital. This man had a history of over 20 suicide attempts, through overdoses, wrist-slashing, and hanging. Many times the attempt appeared to be engineered to fall just short of being successful. He would carefully determine what the lethal dose of the medication was and then take one pill less. He was given to long philosophical discourses on the futility of life and the beauty of death. The last time I saw him he was still "playing with suicide." He eventually shot himself in the stomach on the lawn outside one of the entrances to the hospital. People heard the noise but no one came to investigate, and so, he bled to death.

In discussing suicide among schizophrenic patients,

Farberow, Shneidman and Leonard (1961) describe various personality types. The unaccepting patients refused to gain insight into their own illness though they were very agitated. Tranquilizing drugs appeared to have a calming effect but did not reduce the likelihood of suicide. In fact, they claimed that the medicine may have confronted them with insights that they were incapable of handling, though they appeared more relaxed. They would be given a weekend pass and would commit suicide while out of the hospital. I recall just such a case in which the patient, a thirty-five year-old man, said during a group therapy session that he realized he was suffering from an incurable illness (schizophrenia), and life was hopeless. He was scheduled to go on a weekend pass that day. The group attempted to dissuade him from his negative attitude, but to no avail. I left word for his ward physician that I felt he was actively suicidal and should not be given the pass. The doctor did not receive the message. The patient went home and shot himself.

In determining how to intervene most effectively, one must take into account the significant psychological dynamics of suicide. Farberow (1961) discusses these from the perspective of various personality theories. The Freudian concept of retroflexed rage is one dynamic underlying depression. The importance of hostility as a dynamic cannot be minimized. However, the key to understanding the process lies in understanding the mechanism of dependency. Depression itself is a dependency adaption and the self-directed rage can be seen as a reaction to frustrated dependency. Individuals who become totally dependent on others for their own self-esteem develop self-abnegation which results in death because the person neglects him or herself in pursuit of the esteem of others. Cultural influences enter, in that some religion, government, and other systemized orders have idealized self-abnegation. This is a perfect description of what happened in Jonestown. In dealing with the suicidal patient the therapist must take an exceedingly directive and authoritative role so as to harness the dependency needs, while at the same time not provoking the hostility of the patient by reacting to the latter's hostility. Such a reaction would confirm the patient's conviction of being a hateful person and support that part that wants to break off contact and finish the job of suicide.

In the case of the girl who took the pills and then called me, the goal was a simple one: to get her to agree to a face-to-face contact. The technique was essentially one of seduction, subtly offering gratification of her dependency needs in return for the assignation. She had all of the usual arguments about why she could not meet me. As in most seduction situations, a combination of "sweet talk" and persistence won the day. I was then able to establish contact with the patient in such a way that we could meet face to face. At the meeting it was relatively simple to convince the patient that she really had agreed to see the therapist because she was ambivalent about suicide and was not certain if she really wanted to kill herself. At that point she was willing to let the therapist accompany her to the emergency room to have her stomach pumped. All this took less than 1 hour, and I had medical consultation during that period of time.

When the importance of clarifying the ambivalence in the mind of the patient is considered, one might also come to the conclusion that one of the reasons that the Jonestown massacre occurred was that the system was so devised that a voice of doubt could not be raised. This was one of the functions of the armed guards who dealt most harshly with anyone who chose to contradict the idea being promulgated by the leader of the cult. It is characteristic of the cult that it does not tolerate dissent, which is most conducive to the accomplishment of the suicidal goal. Had it been possible for the voice of dissent to be raised with impunity, it would have created doubt in the minds of a large number of the participants. The ultimate outcome would have been quite different, certainly in terms of the number of people who died.

In the suicidal crisis we must consider that very often the required intervention will be via a telephone contact. Here the skills of the therapist are tested to the greatest degree. The absence of the face-to-face contact makes it possible for there to be misinterpretation of any particular communication, which can lead to termination of the contact and an unhappy outcome. The first task confronting the therapist in the phone contact situation is to keep the patient talking and then assess the lethality of the situation. The second task is to obtain some idea of the particular state of mind or of the diagnostic picture. The task is much different in dealing with one who is severely depressed than in dealing with a schizophrenic or an individual in a state of high panic. All of these will commit suicide, but each will respond differently to the kinds of communications that the therapist is likely to deliver. For example, in the case of the severely depressed individual, the hostility and dependency dynamics are paramount. The therapist, who in his or her zeal to establish control over the situation, acts in an overly demanding way, will very likely evoke severe hostility on the part of the depressed patient. The person might very likely respond with a statement like, "You're just like all the others, you don't really give a damn about me," and hang up.

The therapist, therefore, must project himself or herself as strong enough to accept the dependency needs of the patient, but not so strong as to appear aggressive, and thereby evoke hostility responses.

The case of the panicky patient demands a very different type of response. Here the therapist must project an image that is at once soothing and omnipotent to remove the source of the unbearable panic, thus obviating for the patient the need to escape into the suicidal alternative.

Conclusion

We have touched upon a variety of theoretical approaches to suicide and their implications for intervention. In the process we have briefly discussed the tremendous complexity and infinite variety of behaviors and motivations that may ultimately lead individuals to terminate their own existence. The mental health practitioner who would intervene with potential suicides must realize that one cannot know too much or ever feel too sure of oneself, for sooner or later the therapist will surely hold in his/her hands the most precious possession of another human being, a possession which at that moment that person may desperately wish to discard. And yet, these people may also be relying on the therapist to help them through that crisis period so that they might reach another point in time when they will be in a position to better exercise their own discretion in deciding their future.

REFERENCES

Farberow, N. L., & Shneidman, E. S. (Eds.) *The cry for help.* New York: McGraw-Hill, 1961.

Shneidman, E. S. (Ed.) *Essays in self-destruction.* New York: Science House, 1967.

Shneidman, E. S. (Ed.) *On the nature of suicide.* San Francisco: Jossey-Bass, Inc., 1969.

Chapter 5

THE SPECIAL ROLE OF THE PASTORAL COUNSELOR WITH POTENTIAL SUICIDES

Israel Mowshowitz

One of the most amusing incidents in my more than 4 decades of ministering to the Jewish community was when I received a call from a distraught woman at 1:30 a.m. She explained to me that she could not sleep, that she was depressed, anxious, unnerved, with thoughts of suicide. I suggested to her that she consult her husband who was a prominent psychiatrist. She replied with some indignation: "I would not think of waking up my husband at this hour of the night."

I recall this incident not to evoke sympathy for the rabbi, but rather to illustrate the fact that the first person to whom a potential suicide would turn would probably be his or her clergyperson. This is so for two very important reasons: first, because the clergyperson is always available; you don't have to make an appointment with him or her as you would a psychiatrist or any other person engaged in the mental health field. Second, the clergy do not charge a fee; their services are freely given.

It is precisely because the clergyperson is the first one to become involved with potential suicides and their families that it is all the more important to provide clergy with a basic understanding of how to proceed with a successful intervention in such crisis situations.

Statistical evidence indicates that the number of suicides in our society is alarmingly increasing, especially among young people. But statistics in themselves do not tell the whole story. Gregory Zilboorg maintains that

> . . . Statistical data on suicide as they are compiled today deserve little if any credence. It has been repeatedly pointed out by scientific students of the problem that suicide cannot be subject to statistical evaluation, since all too many suicides are not reported as such. Those who kill themselves through automobile accidents are almost never recorded as suicides. Those who sustain serious injuries during an attempt to commit suicide and die weeks or months later of these injuries or intercurrent infections are never registered as suicides. A great many suicides are concealed by families, and suicidal attempts, no matter how serious, never find their way into the tables of vital statistics. It is obvious that under these circumstances the statistical data available cover the smallest and probably the least representative number of suicides. One is justified, therefore, in discarding them as merely useless in a scientific evaluation of the problem.

Statisticians inform us that some 5,000 young Americans commit suicide every year and that altogether 25,000 Americans commit suicide yearly. This, we must bear in mind, is a minimal figure. By doubling this figure we will be closer to the true state of suicide in America.

Humans are the only creatures aware of their own mortality. They are able to contemplate the past as well as the future, to consider their personal end and to be cognizant of their own death. Walt Whitman put it this way:

I think I could learn to live with animals . . .
They do not sweat and whine about their condition,
They do not lie awake in the dark and weep for their
sins . . .

It is the glory and the agony of human beings that they do sweat and whine about their condition, and they weep for their sins.

Suicide is basically a religious problem. Rollo May defines religion as "the assumption that life has meaning, that it is an 'ultimate concern' (Tillich, cited in May)." A potential suicide is one who has lost all meaning in life. To live means to struggle, to be tested, to be faced with obstacles and to be able to survive difficulties. The Talmud relates that a well known Jewish Sage would always rise before the elderly—even before the heathen elderly—explaining to his students: "How many difficulties these elderly must have overcome in attaining their longevity." To live implies the necessity to suffer and the ability to endure. People are able and willing to suffer and to face up to life's trials provided they see meaning and purpose in life. When these are lost, why endure? Victor Frankl, himself an Auschwitz survivor, noted that the crucial question in the ability to survive was whether the inmate had found purpose in his existential condition. He quotes Neitszche's famous remark to the effect that a person who knows the "why" will be able to endure almost any "how."

Ari Kiev warns us against the tempting assumption that suicides simply "give up" on life, that they are drained of their energy and can no longer resist the death wish. Suicides are not will-less, wandering about aimlessly. They make the choice to do away with themselves and the choice requires energy, will, and courage. They have, as far as we are concerned, made the wrong choice and it is our task to intervene and to direct their energies and will toward making a proper choice, namely to choose to live.

In order for potential suicides to make the choice for life, we must help them to find meaning and purpose in life through their inherent strength and capacities. No person is so unfortunate as to be completely without any redeeming features.

The Bible states that there is not a man who "doeth only good and sinneth not." The reverse is also true. There is not a man who only sinneth and doeth not any good. The potential suicide must be led to see his or her potential for good and for positive purpose of living. The family can be a great help in suicide intervention. Durkheim long ago pointed out that suicide is not a private act; it must be understood in its social contexts. Society, and specifically the family, can do much either to induce or to prevent suicide.

Anne Sexton, a Pulitzer Prize poet, suffered from severe depression which eventually led to her suicide. Expressing the traditional woman's role, she once remarked: "I need my husband and children . . . to tell me who I am." It is the family that defines our personalities and gives us either a feeling of worth or unworthiness. In our relations with the other members of the family we discover who we are. This relationship is a point of reference which helps us to locate ourselves. It must therefore not only be intervention with the potential suicide but also with the family.

How can we recognize a potential suicide? Depression is a sign of alarm. We used to think that childhood is a "golden age," that children do not suffer from depression, that childhood is a happy and carefree period of our lives. We know better now. Depression plagues both young and old although it affects the old much more. It was Thoreau who observed that "most men live lives of quiet desperation." When the depression is deep and renders the individual listless, without will and drive to meet the everyday tasks of life, it is a warning that we may have before us a potential suicide.

Loneliness is a danger signal. Norman Cousins maintains that all man's history is an endeavor to shatter his loneliness. The loner finds life weighing heavily upon him or her. A woman who recently committed suicide wrote in her diary every day the week before: "Nobody called today, nobody called today, nobody called today."

An enterprising college student wrote to a number of prominent persons to ask them what in their opinion was the saddest word in the English vocabulary. One person wrote back that the saddest word was "saddest." Another person wrote that the saddest word was "hopeless." Someone else thought "failure" to be the saddest word. I would nominate for the saddest word the lonely "I."

The loss of a dear one is a danger signal. A man who loses his wife after many years of marriage or a woman who loses her husband—the widow or widower—find themselves with a sudden emptiness, with a void in their lives, with love and emotional attachment loose and nowhere to go. The loss of a child or a father and mother or of a close relative or friend may evoke thoughts of suicide.

Every death that occurs in the family arouses feelings of guilt on the part of the surviving members. There is the popular adage, "If wishes were horses, beggars would ride." Our subconscious aspires to this equestrian status. In any family configuration it is unavoidable that the members occasionally rub each other the wrong way. People who live in close proximity to each other are often impatient and angry with those with whom they share life intimately.

It is unavoidable that in a moment of great anger we would wish our closest and dearest ones dead. When the person towards whom this wish was expressed suddenly dies, we understand logically that this death had nothing to do with our wish. Psychologically, however, we feel guilty. This heavy burden of guilt may lead to contemplation of suicide.

Dramatic changes of status and fortune are a danger signal. It is difficult to accept a fall from affluence to poverty. It induces the feeling in such persons that it is proof of their inadequacy, that they are the cause of their fall. It makes them feel unworthy. But if it is not easy to go from riches to rags, it is sometimes just as difficult to go from rags to riches. A few years ago a young, brilliant actor, Freddie Prinz, had a million dollar a year contract. He was the toast of the entire TV industry. At the height of his career he committed suicide. He had in his brief meteoric career gone, as someone said, from subway to Rolls Royce. It was not an easy transition to make. He had achieved his goal, he "made it" in the entertainment industry; but now that he was successful he had no further goal in life. Life lost meaning.

Retired people who had eminently successful careers and must now adjust to a radically changed life style are prone to thoughts of suicide. Retirement for them is a sign of rejection by society and of their own uselessness. Psychiatrists speak of "pension suicide" when pensioners, after saying a final goodbye to co-workers, leave with their presents and commit suicide. They interpret the company's favor in giving them a generous pension as indicating that they are not needed anymore, that they serve no use nor purpose.

Continuous anger is a danger signal. The wish to express the anger concretely is strong, but there may be no external objects available upon whom to vent one's rage, so the person may therefore turn the aggression upon the self. Karl Menninger cites the example of a teenager who was scolded by his father. He went to the barn and hanged himself. He had really wished to kill his father but perhaps he loved his father too much or perhaps he feared him too much, and he feared the consequences, so he expressed his great rage by killing himself. It was aggression turned inward. In German suicide is called *selbstmord*, self-murder.

Severe illness is a danger signal. A person will sometimes commit "balance-sheet" suicide. He will naturally weigh the reasons for continuing to live and the reasons to terminate life. Such a patient comes to the logical conclusion that the pain, misery, the loss of dignity, and the cost to the family are too much to pay for living.

Role of Clergy

How does the clergyperson intervene in these situations? His or her intervention differs radically from that of the psychiatrist. The psychiatric counselor does not need to reveal a private moral commitment to the patient. To the contrary; it is important that he or she not intrude such positions into the situation. Ethical neutrality is advisable for the psychiatrist. It is impossible and undesirable in religious counselling.

The clergy deal with moral issues which are not a concern of psychotherapy. The psychotherapist's goal is to establish normal mental health and adjustment to society. For the clergy, on the other hand, the goal is to bring about a change in the patient from a state of purposeless living to a meaningful one. The clergy deal with the ultimate concerns of life. Suicides are largely a result of lack of purpose in life, of a sense of loneliness and isolation, a feeling of unworthiness and guilt. This is precisely the province of the clergy. All these questions are basically religious ones.

The clergyperson represents the interpretation of a

world guided by a divine intelligence and the belief that there is a divine meaning in human existence. He or she is committed to the concept of the infinite worth of every individual. The *Mishna* (tractate *Sanhedrin* 37a) explains that the reason God created only one man, Adam, was to teach us that he who saves one human being is as if he had saved the world, and he who causes one human being to perish is as if he had caused the whole world to perish. Every human life is priceless and should be treasured as a gift from God.

Judaism also stresses the need of community. We require a *minyan*, a quorum of 10 in order to pray. We are responsible one for the other. Furthermore, Judaism stresses the uniqueness of every human being. The rabbis tell us (*Sanhedrin* 37a) to note the difference between the Holy One, blessed be He, and a king of flesh and blood. A king of flesh and blood mints coins that are all the same. God, on the other hand, has minted all his children from the same mold—in his own image—and yet each one of them is different and unique. Carlyle expressed it in the following way: "God does not rhyme his children." Every human being is someone special and every human being is needed precisely because of that uniqueness.

Armed with these theological principles the clergyperson is eminently prepared successfully to intervene with potential suicides and their families. The very least that a clergyperson can do is to listen. The wise King Solomon observed: "If a person has a worry in his heart let him share it." The opportunity to talk to someone who lends a sympathetic ear will bring some measure of relief.

The clergyperson is also in the position to ease the turmoil in the troubled soul by pointing out that such feelings are not unusual, that there are many who suffer as this individual does. This may somewhat lift the burden of self-condemnation. It can be pointed out that sin is universal. One of the Five Books of Moses is devoted to what a sinful person should do to find reconciliation with God and his fellowman. It will be a comfort to distressed people to realize that they are not alone in their feelings of unworthiness and inadequacy; that they are members of the great company of sinners. The Day of Atonement is not just for some people but for everyone. Such an understanding will have the effect of alleviating the feelings of guilt in the troubled person.

The clergy can also address themselves effectively to the need for a love object to replace the one lost through death or abandonment. The *Kaddish,* the prayer in honor of the departed, for example, is always recited with a *minyan* in a religious quorum. It constitutes a pledge on the part of the surviving children to fill the void in the community that was left by their father's or mother's death. The mourners are welcomed into the synagogue to the Sabbath services with the words "May God comfort you among all those who mourn for Zion and Jerusalem." Judaism calls upon the mourners to attach their love to the needs of the community, to the needs of their people, to an ideal which was close to the heart of the departed. The clergy can make the mourners feel that they are part of a religious fellowship bound together by a common tradition and common concerns.

The clergy can also stress the teaching of Judaism about God's compassion and forgiveness. The basic theme of Judaism is not so much that people sin, but that having sinned, the way is always open to repentance. Jewish tradition does not recognize a point of no return in human life.

The clergy are in an excellent position to educate the family to the problems confronting potential suicides, to make them feel needed, loved, and accepted. The Hungarian psychoanalyst, Sandor Ferenczi, observed about families: "They want to love one another, but they do not know how." The clergy can help the family to become more supportive of each other and not to be afraid to express their care, their love, and their concern for one another. Potential suicides may get the impression that they are being rejected because the members of their family do not know how to express the need that they feel for them. One of the most powerful supports that can be given to a potential suicide is the feeling of being really needed. When a clergyperson confronts a family in bereavement and finds an onset of deep depression at the loss, his or her most effective appeal is to call attention to the need that the surviving members have for each other and the comfort and strength that they can give to one another.

But how about "balance-sheet" suicide? If a logical reckoning of the objective circumstances leads to the conclusion that suicide is the better way, how is one to handle such a case?

Recently Rabbi Yechiel Orenstein was confronted with a woman member of his congregation who had terminal cancer from which she was in constant discomfort and pain. She attempted suicide a number of times. After the last attempt and the long session of counseling with the woman, he came home to relate to his family how frustrated he felt at not knowing what to say to this "balance-sheet" suicide. His fourteen year-old daughter, whose ambition it is to be a rabbi, then suggested the following approach: the woman must be reminded that life is not our own but a gift from God. When someone received a gift, even though it is not to one's liking, one does not throw it back into the face of the giver. One must accept life and live it to one's best even when life is not what one would like it to be. She would further point out to the woman to think about what kind of legacy she would be leaving her children and grandchildren. Her suicide would tell them that when life becomes rough the thing to do is to cop out, to give up. Surely, this is not the kind of a legacy anyone would want to leave for the future generation.

This indeed is sound counseling. Life is a gift from God. Suicide is not a personal, private act. Life is not ours to take, and our own lives are intertwined intimately with and affect the lives of many others. The potential suicide must be led to understand that in the struggle between the will to live and the will to die, this individual is not the only one involved.

B. Life Cycle

INTRODUCTION

The chapters under this heading discuss detection, prevention, and intervention with potential suicides of various ages. The themes that were delineated in part I of this section can be found in most stages of human development. Depression, rage, loss, and hopelessness characterize all suicidal individuals; prevention requires the assistance of social groups, significant others, skillful therapists, and pastoral counselors. The particular feature of the following chapters is their special emphasis on issues pertaining to suicidal children, adolescents, and youth, and the terminally ill who generally comprise the adult and aged population.

Chapter 6, *Recognizing and Treating Suicidal Youngsters*, dispels misconceptions regarding the absence of suicidal inclinations in children. It claims that many suicides are actually disguised as accidents and many therapists deny that children can be suicidal. Practitioners should be sensitive to numerous clues. The most specific affective parameter associated with suicidal behavior among children is depression. Its symptoms may be hyperactivity, delinquency, learning disabilities, and overt sadness. The affective state of other family members, particularly depression and aggressive behavior by parents, correlates with high risk in children. The death of a parent may cause inordinate stress to the young child which may later be expressed as anxiety and aggression. Suicidal tendencies are not constant states but appear and reappear at different times. Prevention should strive to protect the child from future harm by intervening with the child and the family, alone and together. Family interventions must be geared to enhancing communication, and must include a system for follow-up.

Chapter 7, *Some Special Aspects of Suicide in Adolescents and Youth* makes a strong case for the propensity of adolescents to commit suicide. In her review of adolescent development, the author cites the psychological stresses, bodily changes and sexual tensions, communications problems with parents, intensification of aggressive impulses, enormous creativity, and vulnerability to depression and anxiety that typically characterize this age group. Some specific precipitants are: problems in families, particularly the absence or death of a parent, breakup of an important romance, physical illness, homosexual longings, and alienation from parents.

Warning signals such as hostility and interest in another person's suicide are discussed. Assessment of suicidal youngsters includes the ideation, structure, method, and setting of the plan. Among numerous intervention modes, it is suggested that the youth be hospitalized on a short-term basis if the symptoms are acute. Otherwise, empathy, concern, availability, and posing as a role model should ideally characterize the quality of the relationship. The therapist should engage significant others in the youth's environment, most notably the family, as part of the support system. By way of prevention, health classes dealing with suicide should be established in educational and social institutions, and hot-lines be provided in the community.

Chapter 8, *Adolescent Suicide: Prevention and Treatment,*

was contributed by a professor of nursing from the perspective of the health provider and the health team. After brief citations of cues to adolescent suicide which reinforce and expand those of the previous chapter, the author focuses on the functions of the health care system, specifically the hospital, after the adolescent's admission. Hospitalization is an intense crisis for the teenager and his/her family. The health team needs to be aware of this fact, sensitive to their own attitudes toward suicide, and strive to establish a relationship with the youngster that is warm, understanding, personal, and empathic; build a sense of trust that contributes to a feeling of self-worth; include family and close friends, "significant others," in the treatment process, and use various community resources such as temporary foster care and crisis intervention centers for psychological and physical supports. The issues are addressed in a straightforward manner and positive feelings for the adolescent are encouraged.

Chapter 9, *Suicidal Ideation in Terminally Ill Patients and their Families,* is included in the *Life Cycle* section because terminal illness generally afflicts the adult and aged populations in our society. It is this special factor in the etiology of suicide that comes under scrutiny because it is generally hushed up by doctors and patients and their families. The factors that lead the terminally ill to contemplate suicide are intense and chronic pain, the perception that one is a burden to one's family and to oneself, the need to gain conrol over one's life cycle by controlling the circumstances of death, and attention-seeking behavior. Family members' suicidal ideation needs to be monitored at the same time as the patient's. The therapist should be attuned to the method selected, the circumstances planned, and other indications such as writing a will. In his/her interventions, the therapist stresses the normalcy of these thoughts, distinguishes between ideation and behavior, and deals with

the ensuing guilt over the thought of suicide. Pastoral counselors and family members are significant persons who
should be enlisted in the patient's struggle.

Chapter 6

RECOGNIZING AND TREATING SUICIDAL YOUNGSTERS

Cynthia R. Pfeffer

The issues pertinent to suicidal behavior of children and adolescents is a new frontier for child psychiatrists, pediatricians, school professionals, and parents. It has only been in the last decade and a half that the psychiatric literature has devoted greater attention to the emergent crises of suicidal children and adolescents (Mattsson et al., 1969; Paulson, et al., 1978; Pfeffer et al., 1979; Pfeffer et al., 1980; Toolan, 1962). Remarkably, this phenomenon has been overlooked because of several perpetuated misconceptions.

One misconception is that children and some adolescents are too young and immature to be able to initiate a method that might cause their own death. It is thought that youngsters lack the physical skill, the cognitive abilities, and the sense of careful planning that are necessary for carrying out a self-destructive act. However, it is a common clinical observation that children and adolescents are capable of inflicting life-endangering harm upon themselves (Pfeffer, 1978; Pfeffer, 1980). Often these children only miraculously survive the effects of their actions. The example of one ten year-old boy dramatically illustrates this fact. The child was hospitalized on a psychiatric inpatient unit after spending 2 months in a pediatric ward for treatment of serious multiple injuries that resulted from his suicidal actions. The child had jumped out of the sixth floor window of his apartment house. It was remarkable that he survived. His life was saved when he hit a clothesline that deflected his fall and subsequently caused him to land in some bushes rather than on the concrete pavement. However, he sustained multiple fractures and severe head injuries.

Another misconception is that young children are unable to understand the consequences of their actions. It is thought that children under the age of twelve are often unable to comprehend concepts of death. Specifically it is believed that children do not recognize that death is final. A consequence of this belief is that it has influenced thinking about the most appropriate definition of suicidal behavior for youngsters. The argument put forth is that if a child is unable fully to understand that death is final, it is not possible to catalogue a child's self-destructive behavior as suicidal because suicidal behavior implies a definite knowledge that death is final. Therefore, it is asserted that one cannot cite suicide as the cause of death in children until the children are mature enough fully to comprehend the finality of death. It must be emphasized that this idea stems from theoretical and developmental models which have not been fully explored by means of empirical studies. In fact, there are very few systematic empirical studies that evaluate normal children and suicidal children's ideas and beliefs about death. Such research is urgently needed. In part, because of these beliefs, the Office of National Vital

Statistics does not catalogue suicide as a cause of death in children under the age of ten years.

Another issue that needs to be addressed is the documentation of death caused by accident in these children. It is widely recognized that accidents are among the leading causes of death in youngsters. Therefore, it may be postulated that a sizeable percentage of reported accidents in children may have been caused by the self-destructive tendencies of these children. Because of this possibility, extensive clinical research is necessary to evaluate the relations between accidental death and potentially suicidal deaths of children.

Other reasons that suicidal behavior among children and adolescents has been underestimated have been attributed to restraint from societal pressures, political concerns, religious and cultural dogma, and the fear of family stigma. Because of these taboos, suicidal deaths frequently may be disguised and reported as accidental or resulting from other causes. These issues which perpetuate the closeting of children's suicidal behavior have long-standing historical roots. However, only by sensitizing the public to childhood suicidal phenomena, its recognition and modes of intervention and prevention, will fears and inhibitions regarding discussion, evaluation, and means of deterring this type of behavior be provided.

A final factor in the limited recognition of suicidal behavior among children is the common reaction of professionals who work with suicidal youngsters. Extreme anxiety is often generated, not only by the crisis situation with its impending threat of death of a child, but also by the clinician's own inner perceptions, fantasies, and fears regarding death. These feelings and thoughts are vividly stimulated when one works with children who wish to kill themselves. One's reactions to life and death situations become heightened. If conscious and unconscious conflicts exist, one's defenses to ward off direct involvement with such events may be mobilized. One common defense is a high degree of denial in recognizing the subtle clues to potential suicidal behavior of children. Carried to the extreme, there may be denial that a child has actually threatened or attempted to take his or her life. The seriousness of suicidal behavior is often minimized. These responses are prevalent not only for clinicians but also for parents who tend to overlook the dramatic pleas for help inherent in their child's self-destructive tendencies. Because of this minimization of the danger to potentially suicidal children, these children are often not brought immediately for psychiatric consultation. Instead, parents often believe that the situation will soon remedy itself. Therefore, appropriate sensitization of the community to the needs of recognizing and intervening with potentially suicidal youngsters may diminish the strong tendencies of denial regarding suicidal behavior among children.

The Extent of the Problem

Suicidal behavior among children and adolescents is a definitive national mental health problem. The suicide rate for adolescents is remarkably high. For example, during the last 2 decades, the suicide rate has more than doubled (Frederick, 1979; Holinger, 1978). Suicide is now one of the leading causes of death in young adults between ages sixteen and twenty years. However, the documentation that exists for completed suicide among children under the age of twelve years seems to indicate that this phenomenon is relatively rare (Shaffer, 1974). However, it must be emphasized that the statistics are actually often inaccurate, and, in fact, not kept. Therefore, extensive research in evaluating the cause of children's death is warranted. This may provide a more accurate overview of the rate of suicide among children under the age of twelve years.

In contrast to completed suicide rates, it is now widely recognized that suicidal ideas, threats, and attempts among children between the ages of six and twelve years are relatively common (Pfeffer, 1979; Pfeffer, 1980, Shaffer, 1974). Furthermore, suicidal children and adolescents use a wide variety of methods to inflict harm. The methods include ingesting harmful substances, jumping from heights, drowning, burning, stabbing, and hanging (Paulson, 1978; Pfeffer, 1979; Pfeffer, 1980). Although among children under twelve years of age there does not seem to be a difference in the types of methods used by boys or girls, there do seem to be distinctions in the types of methods used by boy and girl adolescents. For example, adolescent girls tend to ingest poisonous substances more frequently than adolescent boys (Holinger, 1978). However, adolescent boys tend to use more violent methods such as hanging, stabbing, and jumping from heights more frequently than adolescent suicidal girls.

Clues for Recognition of Suicidal Behavior Among Youngsters

Much more research is necessary to evaluate the factors that may increase risk for suicidal actions in children and adolescents. Many parameters have been implicated but they have not been sufficiently systematically studied. Many hypotheses have been generated which were based on individual case studies. The conclusions from these studies must be confirmed by means of systematic study of large numbers of suicidal youngsters.

One observation about suicidal behavior is that such behavior in children and adolescents is an impulsive action. However, this conclusion must be seriously challenged because while the action may appear to be impulsive, on more careful study of the child and the circumstances, it is noted that the child has been enduring chronic extreme external and intrapsychic stress, stimulation, and pressure. Therefore, the following clarification is necessary: although suicidal behavior may appear to be impulsive, it is actually the result of long-standing stresses on the child. Therefore, in understanding the clues that may alert one to potential suicidal behavior of children and adolescents, one must evaluate the youngster's history, environment, and current level of functioning. For example, a stress at an earlier phase of development may under certain circumstances stimulate overwhelming and unbearable feelings that may propel a youngster towards suicidal behavior. Therefore, if a boy or girl lost both parents at seven years of age, this trauma may be a nucleus of vulnerability to stress that may be encountered at a later stage of the child's life. Another example is that if an adolescent has to leave home for school, previous vulnerability to loss and separation may hamper the adolescent's ability to endure these changes in his or her life. It must be underscored that the suicidal phenomenon must be understood in the context of the child's entire life history.

Certain factors are specifically related to suicidal behavior of youngsters. These factors have been observed in the histories of large numbers of potentially suicidal children. Furthermore, in addition to the specific factors associated with childhood suicidal behavior, there are other more general parameters that may increase a child's vulnerability to various types of psychopathology. Some of the more general parameters are overwhelming problems within the family such as violence, death, separation, divorce, and illness. Other general factors are vulnerability due to the child's constitutional, temperamental, and developmental level of functioning.

Specific Clues to Suicidal Behavior

The most specific affective parameter associated with suicidal behavior among young people is depression. Many studies have shown that suicidal youngsters exhibit signs of depression (Mattsson, 1968; Paulson, 1978; Pfeffer, 1979; Pfeffer, 1980). However, there is controversy about how to diagnose depression in children and adolescents. In fact, there is even more controversy about whether depression in children and adolescents actually exists. Some clinicians believe that depression cannot be diagnosed in children and adolescents (Rochlin, 1965). This is because these clinicians believe that youngsters have not matured sufficiently to be vulnerable to superego stresses and guilt that is associated with an onset of depressive reactions. However, more recent empirical studies indicate that depression in children and adolescents does exist as an entity (Carlson & Cantwell, 1980; Cytryn et. al., 1980). However, it still remains to be further clarified as to what signs and symptoms constitute and appropriate diagnosis of depression in youngsters. There are some who believe that depression may be masked by many types of symptom pictures (Glaser, 1965; Toolan, 1975). Such symptomatology may include hyperactivity, delinquency, hypochrondriasis, learning disabilities, assaultive behavior, and overt sadness.

Other researchers prefer to diagnose the signs and symptoms of depression in children and adolescents in a more restricted way. These researchers contend that the signs and symptoms of childhood depression are similar to the signs and symptoms of depression among adults (Carlson, 1980; Cytryn, 1980; Puig-Antich, 1978). Furthermore, these signs and symptoms of dysphoric states should exist for at least 2 weeks' duration. Among the signs and symptoms of dysphoria are change in appetite, either an increase or decrease of food intake, sleep distrubances, such as inability to fall asleep, inability to sleep through the night, early morning waking, or inability to wake up in the morning. Other associated signs and symptoms are change in activity level, ranging from hyperactivity to hypomotility, apathy, lethargy, increased social withdrawal, feelings of sadness, crying spells, change in physiological functioning, and specific themes of helplessness, hopelessness, worthlessness, and thoughts that life is not worth living. It has been shown that these signs and symptoms can be readily observed both in children and adolescents.

The knowledge gained by these studies is useful for educating the community to the specific signs and symptoms of depression in children and adolescents. The dissemination of such knowledge may be one step towards prevention of potentially suicidal behavior in young people. However, it must be noted that not all depressed youngsters become suicidal. Additional investigations are urgently needed to understand what types of differences exist among depressed children. Furthermore, although depression is a main affective state that is correlated to suicidal behavior, other affective states such as anxiety and aggression must be investigated with regard to suicidal behavior.

Another specific correlate to childhood suicidal behavior involves the affective state of other family members. That is, depression and suicidal behavior among the parents is another parameter that highly correlates with high risk for suicidal behavior of children and adolescents (Pfeffer, 1979; Pfeffer, 1980). It may be hypothesized that youngsters identify with the affective states of their parents. In this way, depression may be a primary mode of enhancing the affective ties between parents and children. Likewise, witnessing suicidal behavior in a parent may desensitize the child so that the child has minimal deterrent mechanisms against suicidal behavior. Therefore, if a child perceives that a parent copes with intense stress by means of suicidal behavior, it may be easier for such a child under stress to respond to pressure by means of suicidal action. This may be a primary mechanism in which suicidal children identify with their parents' modes of coping with pressure.

Another family parameter that deserves more attention and investigation is violent and aggressive behavior within families. Researchers indicated that abusive and violent behavior among parents may enhance the potential for self-destructive behavior among children (Green, 1968). Such self-destructive behavior may include head banging, hair-pulling, nail-biting, self-scratching, and suicidal threats and attempts. However, additional investigations are needed to understand the interactive effects between violence and self-destructive behaviors among children.

Another important parameter specifically associated with childhood suicidal behavior is the child's understanding, preoccupations, experiences, and concepts about death. Studies have shown that suicidal children often believe that death is a pleasant state and that death is reversible (Pfeffer, 1979; Pfeffer, 1980; Orbach & Glaubman, 1979). Such beliefs diminish the deterrent capacity of the child toward suicidal action. For example, if a child thinks that death is reversible and that it may lead to a pleasant state in which stress is diminished, the child may actively plan a means to ensure that he or she dies. Paradoxically, although suicidal children may consider death to be a temporary and agreeable state, this may not be the child's concept of death when not in a suicidal state. It must be emphasized that in children under twelve years of age, concepts of death are fluid and not fixed. At a given moment, a child may fully understand that death is irreversible, but at another time, when under extreme stress, the child may lose this understanding and believe that death is temporary and reversible.

An example suffices to illustrate this point. Nathan was an eight year-old boy who was admitted to the child inpatient unit of a local hospital because of his suicidal tendencies. His family was stressed by marital discord. Nathan found solace in the company of his maternal grandfather. Nathan loved his grandfather, who unfortunately had been ill for some time. During the initial phases of Nathan's hospitalization, he was able to say that death was final and that he felt that death was not pleasant. Unfortunately, Nathan's grandfather died while Nathan was in the hospital. After the death, Nathan was confused about death. He emphatically stated that some day his grandfather would return and that life still existed after one died. Furthermore, Nathan believed that his grandfather went to heaven and in fact he wished that he join his grandfather. Yet, if Nathan was asked about animals dying, he was able appropriately to state that death is final.

This poignant case illustrates the complexities of children's understanding and experience with death. Therefore, it behooves clinicians who evaluate potentially suicidal children to ask specifically about the child's concepts about death. If, for example, a child believes that death is temporary and that it may lead to a present situation, the potential for suicidal behavior may be increased. The deterrent barriers for suicidal action are weakened by such concepts of death.

Another issue pertinent to the recognition of potentially suicidal behavior of children and adolescents is that suicidal behavior is not necessarily a constant state. Suicidal tendencies may last for only moments, hours, days, or weeks. It may appear and disappear. Therefore, at a given moment, a child or adolescent may not appear to be suicidal, but within a short period of time may actively demonstrate suicidal impulses. This fluctuation must be emphasized and the difficulties of fully evaluating the potential for suicidal behavior must be stressed. Only by careful intensive observation of the child and the complex situation in which the child lives, will a clinician be able appropriately to evaluate a child's potential for suicidal action. Needless to say, because of the difficulties of evaluating the potential for suicidal action, clinicians' anxieties are enhanced. Often, clinicians must deal with ambiguity and confusion.

Children are often unable to speak about their wishes, fantasies, and feelings. Therefore, clues to suicidal potential must be sought in observations of a child's behavior. Clues may be obtained by observation of the quality of a child's play. Investigations have indicated that certain parameters may point out a tendency toward suicidal behavior (Pfeffer, 1979). For example, repetivite destruction of a play object may be a clue to potential suicidal behavior. A child who breaks his toys or throws his toys out the window may be a risk for potential suicidal behavior. Another play clue to suicidal behavior may be the repetitive theme of falling or loss. A child may play repeatedly that he is falling from the roof of a building. Another clue may be identifying with superheros and a playing out of dangerous and reckless themes. Therefore, a child who plays that he is Superman and attempts to fly out the window may be at risk for suicidal behavior.

Main Principles of Intervention for Suicidal Youngsters

When a child is suicidal, the intervention techniques must be flexible and varied. A first major concern is to protect the child from future harm. This necessitates intervention not only with the child but also with the child's family. Assessment of the risk for future harm must be made rapidly and immediately. It may be necessary to consider psychiatric hospitalization of the youngster. The advantage of this is to ensure round the clock observation and immediate intervention. Hospitalization also provides a neutral situation in which to work on underlying factors that promote suicidal responses. In contrast to psychiatric hospitalization, outpatient treatment of acutely suicidal children may be undertaken if it seems clear to the therapist, to the child, and to the family that the child is safe from future harm.

All interventions with potentially suicidal children begin by determining an accurate diagnosis which consists of two components. First there is the diagnosis of the degree of potential for suicidal action. Second, there is the diagnosis of underlying psychopathology of the child. For example, if a child has an attention deficit disorder, interventions must also be geared at remediating such a disorder. Likewise, if the child shows psychotic tendencies, appropriate interventions for the child's psychosis must be organized.

A basic premise of intervention with potentially suicidal children and adolescents is that suicidal behavior is the signal of the child's stress and also of underlying family distress. Therefore the intervention should focus on the child and family, and with the child's parents alone. Flexibility of intervention strategy is necessary. The purpose of intervention is to allow for open communication among family members so that they may discover the types of stresses that prompted their child's suicidal action.

Family interventions must be geared to enhancing communication. It must be acknowledged that the child's suicidal behavior is an indicator of difficulties within the entire family. The suicidal child must be looked upon as a signal of other difficulties among the family members. Furthermore, suicidal behavior is a process that is determined not only by one individual within the family, but by a complex state of interactions among the family members.

Finally, intervention of suicidal children is a long-range endeavor that must include a system for follow-up. This will ensure that necessary interventions are available if the child becomes acutely suicidal again.

Summary

Suicidal behavior among children and adolescents is now a national mental health problem. Appropriate methods of diagnosis and intervention must be developed. Such parameters as depression in the child and parents, parental suicidal behavior, and the child's distorted concepts about death, specifically correlate with potential for suicidal behavior among youngsters. Interventions must focus on protecting the youngster from harm and on unraveling the underlying chronic interpersonal and family stresses. Incorporating all family members in the treatment is required. Planning the interventions so that a long term process can evolve is necessary in treating a suicidal child.

REFERENCES

Carlson, G. A., & Cantwell, D. P. Unmasking masked depression in children and adolescents. *American Journal of Psychiatry*, 1980, *137*, 445–449.

Cytryn L. McKnew, D. H., Jr., & Bunney, W. E. Diagnosis of depression in children: A reassessment. *American Journal of Psychiatry*, 1980, *137*, 22–25.

Frederick, C. J. Current trends in suicidal behavior in the United States. *American Journal of Psychotherapy*, 1979, *32*, 172–200.

Glaser, K. Attempted suicide in children and adolescents: Psychodynamic observations. *American Journal of Psychotherapy*. 1965, *19*, 220–227.

Green, A. H. Self destructive behavior in battered children. *American Journal of Psychiatry*, 1968, *135*, 579–582.

Holinger, P. C. Adolescent suicide: An epidemiological study of recent trends. *American Journal of Psychiatry*, 1978, *135*, 754–756.

Mattsson, A., Hawkins, J. W., & Seese, L. R. Suicidal behavior as a child psychiatric emergency. *Archives of General Psychiatry*, 1969, *20*, 100–109.

Orbach I., & Glaubman H. The concept of death and suicidal behavior in young children. Three case studies. *Journal of American Academy of Child Psychiatry*, 1979, *18*, 668–678.

Paulson, M. J., Stone, D., & Sposto, R. Suicide potential and behavior in children ages 4 to 12. *Suicide & Life Threatening Behavior*, 1978, *8*, 225–242.

Pfeffer, C. R. Clinical observations of play of suicidal latency age children, *Suicide & Life Threatening Behavior*, 1979, *9*, 235–244.

Pfeffer, C. R., Conte, H. R., Plutchik, R., & Jerrett, I. Suicidal behavior in latency age children: An empirical study. *Journal of American Academy of Child Psychiatry*, 1979, *18*, 679–692.

Pfeffer, C. R., Conte, H. R., Plutchik, R., & Jerrett, I. Suicidal behavior in latency age children: An empirical study: An outpatient population *Journal of American Academy of Child Psychiatry*, 1980, *19*, 703–710.

Puig-Antich, J., Blau, S., et al. Prepubertal major depressive disorders: A pilot study, *Journal of American Academy of Child Psychiatry*, 1978, *17*, 695–707.

Rochlin, G. N. *Griefs and discontents: The forces of change.* Boston: Little, Brown & Co., 1965.

Shaffer, D. Suicide in childhood and early adolescents. *Journal of Child Psychology and Psychiatry*, 1974, *15*, 275–191.

Toolan, J. M. Depression in children and adolescents, *American Journal of Orthopsychiatry*, 1962, *32*, 404–415.

Toolan, J. M. Suicide in children and adolescents, *American Journal of Psychotherapy*, 1975, *29*, 339–334.

Chapter 7

SOME SPECIAL ASPECTS OF SUICIDE IN ADOLESCENCE AND YOUTH

Russett P. Feldman

I

The suicide and attempted suicide rates of adolescents have escalated to an alarming degree recently. Specifically, the number of suicidal deaths in the fifteen to twenty-four year-old age group increased from 4/100,000 in 1957 to 13.6/100,000 in 1977. Estimates are that there may be as many as 200 attempts for every successful suicide in youth of this age. Moreover, one of every 200 adolescents will make a serious suicide attempt. Nearly 50 percent of all attempters are less than thirty years old. These statistics become even more disturbing when one considers that they are only estimates: suicide attempts are often unreported and many deaths termed "accidental" actually may have been intentional.

At present, suicide as a cause of death of fifteen to twenty-four year-olds ranks second only to "accidents." These statistics demonstrate that anyone dealing with youth, whether it be on a professional, familial, or casual basis, understand and detect the potential suicide attempter and intervene in a meaningful way.

II

To do so, it is necessary to understand the nature of typical adolescents and their environment. Adolescence begins with puberty, the onset of which occurs at different times in each individual. Sexual urges become pressing. These changes cause adolescents to be uncomfortable with themselves and with others. The profound bodily changes associated with adolescence cause feelings of embarrassment, confusion, jealousy, and self-consciousness.

At the same time, their parents, who recognize these changes, may also react with embarrassment, jealousy, and fear. Seeing their pubertal child reawakens in parents feelings from their own adolescent turmoil and struggle with sexuality. Because of parents' anxiety over unresolved feelings, they cannot be as available to their children. Communication between the generations may therefore become distant.

That communication may be further strained because adolescents with their new bodies begin to re-evaluate childhood prohibitions about sex. Experimentation with masturbation and homosexuality occur, but not without feelings of guilt and shame. Parents who have difficulty with their own sexuality may be unconsciously frightened and may wish to protect their adolescents, and therefore, may fail to be candid about sexual knowledge.

Adolescence involves reawakening of the oedipal conflicts of childhood in the context of new sexual development. Sexual wishes toward the parent of the opposite sex and fear of the parent of the same sex cause anxiety and embarrassment and add further to the alienation of the generations. Partly to compensate for this alienation, adolescents with their pressing sexual urges propel themselves toward peer sexual experimentation.

Along with the reorganization of their sexual urges is the intensification of aggressive impulses as well as conflicts between dependency needs and desires to be independent. Adolescents may rebel in an effort to assert their autonomy. At the same time, they long for parental advice to help curb their new, uncontrollable impulses. Many parents interpret this rebellion personally and do not understand its derivations. As a result, they may become angry, resentful, and more unavailable to their teenagers, who need them more than ever.

Because of disillusionment in their parents who are seemingly not understanding, adolescents look for new role models such as teachers and sports figures. However, these role models are bound to have imperfections too; therefore adolescents never feel comfortable with any consistent authority. They nevertheless need to feel committed to some authority. This accounts for the importance of peer groups. In order to belong to these peer groups, individuals must prove themselves, sometimes by using drugs or alcohol. Such abuse may generate feelings of guilt, depression, and anxiety.

Related to the striving for independence and growing disillusionment with their parents is the enormous creativity of adolescence. New ideas arise in the context of pressing emotions and feelings. However, adolescents' thinking processes are in the transition from the concrete to the abstract. This results in a peculiar paradox in which adolescents can think about death, for example, but do not understand the permanence of it. Adolescents are also students, and in the classic literature, death is a major dramatic theme.

Action and movement are hallmarks of adolescence. Every act seems fraught with urgency and ambivalence. Adolescents are impulsive because the emotional changes within them are so sudden and overpowering and because they are so ambivalent. However, the development of controls lag behind the surge in impulses. Failure to control those impulses cause adolescents to suffer a loss of self-esteem. Parents may confuse this with unreliability and may fail to understand their son or daughter. At the same time, the activity of teenagers reminds parents of their own decline, which adds to parents' resentment.

In sum, adolescence is a tumultuous period in which there are new overpowering emotional and physical changes: rebelliousness and the need to belong, creativity, transition to mature thinking, impulsivity, and ambivalence. At a time when these changes are so overwhelming, alienation from parents occurs. These unique aspects cause the adolescent to be especially vulnerable to depression and anxiety—frequent precursors to suicidal behavior.

III

Yet not all adolescents are suicidal: certain adolescents have a higher risk of suicide because of added stress during a period when *normally* they experience multiple changes.

Adolescents who have physical illnesses or handicaps are especially vulnerable to feelings of low self-esteem and depression. Since bodily changes are so conspiciuous and foci of attention and since movement and energy are the norms, adolescents who differ in these respects may become outcasts. This additional alienation from their peer group places these teenagers at a higher risk for depression and suicide.

Similarly, adolescents who find themselves with marked homosexual longings feel estranged, ashamed, and more isolated than others. This isolation and alienation at a time when it is so important to belong to a group also lends itself to depression and the risk of suicide.

Because sexual feelings and wishes to belong to a group are such urgent needs, romantic liaisons become a socially acceptable way to relate in a group. Often suicide attempts occur in the context of a breakup of an important romance. In addition, a teenager who becomes pregnant feels more isolated, fearful, humiliated, and depressed. With the alienation from parents characteristic of this stage of life, the teenager may feel that the only solution is suicide.

Adolescents who are suicidal often come from families in which there was death of a parent during their childhood. Suicidal adolescents often have a neglectful, a rejecting, or a psychiatrically ill parent, a parent who committed suicide, or parents who are divorced or separated. These adolescents may blame themselves for their parents' unavailability and may harbor feelings that they must be unworthy for their parents not to care. At the same time, these parents often have unresolved dependency needs and lean on their children for emotional sustenance. Because adolescents are already struggling with their own dependency needs, they may feel guilty, angry, and overwhelmed.

These feelings of being isolated, humiliated, angry, guilty, and depressed often are overwhelming during this stage of emotional turmoil. Because the adolescent is a creature of action more than of thought, the outlet for these emotions may be suicide attempts. Curiously, the motivation for suicide gestures and attempts often is not the wish to die. The most common motivating factors include the wish to alter an intolerable situation and relieve painful feelings, the wish to join a dead relative or friend to lessen isolation and provide comfort, the wish to retaliate, and the wish to gain affection and sympathy. These motivations reflect the immaturity in adolescents' thinking processes; they feel that their death will bring about a positive change and that they will benefit from that change.

IV

Most adolescent suicide attempters have personality disorders and not psychotic mental illnesses. Only 10 to 20 percent of suicidal adolescents are psychotic, most of them schizophrenics. Among mentally ill adolescents, only a minority are suicidal. However, the depressive spectrum is commonly found in suicidal adolescents. Depression may be manifested by sadness, hopelessness, helplessness, guilt, anxiety, emptiness, irritability, and agitation or lethargy and apathy. There may be changes in eating or sleeping patterns: overeating or anorexia, hypersomnia or insomnia. There may be social withdrawal and isolation. Adolescents may abuse drugs and/or alcohol, often in an attempt to "medicate" their depression.

Suicidal attempters are more hostile than others and are more apt to generate hostility in others because of their dependency and immaturity. They often are poorly able to verbalize their emotional experiences.

Adolescents who are seemingly accident-prone may be careless with their lives because of underlying suicidal fantasies. Seventy-nine percent of those who kill themselves have tried at least one time before. Those who threaten suicide or have made a gesture are at high risk, especially in the 2 years following the first gesture or attempt.

Interest in another person's suicidal ideation or questions about death and afterlife, when it is a sudden philosophical change or when it is of an obsessive quality, are warning signals. Interest in the legal disposition of personal property should alert people to the possibilities of suicidal rumination. When an adolescent gives away a prized possession, he or she may be finalizing a plan for suicide.

The sudden uplifting of a severe depression may signify a plan for suicide. Suicide in this instance may represent a release from an unbearable emotional state, and therefore, suicide plans may actually bring about relief from depression. Moreover, studies have shown that most depressed patients who commit suicide do so 3 months after they have begun to improve because they have regained some of the energy and organization necessary to put their plans into action.

V

The assessment of the suicidal adolescent includes many of the same parameters as in the assessment of any suicidal person. One must assess the actual ideation, the structure of the plan if there is one, the lethality of the method, and the setting of the attempt. Of crucial importance is the understanding of the acute precipitant crisis and the motive behind the suicidal thoughts. One must evaluate the adolescent's support system and family situation. The alienation between adolescents and their parents make teenagers particularly vulnerable and if one only evaluates the presenting adolescent, one is missing the crucial contextual understanding.

After the clinician assess these factors, he or she must decide on a course of action. Short-term hospitalization may be necessary to separate a suicidal adolescent who lives with a disturbed, nonsupportive family. In this case, the hospital provides safety and allows the clinician further to evaluate the family. Hospitalization may also be beneficial if the youth is psychotic or has a major depressive disorder: a hospital may provide a milieu for antipsychotic or antidepressant medication. Its staff could attend to the increased dependency needs found in these conditions.

The majority of adolescents, however, do not require hospitalization. They should be seen in a crisis-intervention type of therapy, where the focus of the sessions should be on the acute situation which has contributed to the suicidal behavior. The therapist should be active, friendly, and concerned, and should try to engage the adolescent as quickly as possible. Adolescents often are difficult to engage, but if the therapist is accepting of the adolescent's feelings, and is firm but supportive and interested, he or she may win the youth's confidence. The therapist must be available to the adolescent and must follow up on any missed appointments in an attempt to communicate concern. The therapist must make use of the adolescent's search for a role model and hero by offering him or herself and thus making it likely that the adolescent will invest him or her with that role.

The youth must be allowed to ventilate personal feelings, and if depressed, must be reassured that the depression will pass in time. The therapist should make conscious the ambivalence about dying, and should not hesitate to emphasize the irreversibility of death. In short, the adolescent must be persuaded that suicide is a futile way of communicating distress or of promoting change. Instead, verbal means of expression should be encouraged. Nevertheless, the therapist must continually monitor the adolescent's suicide potential. The therapist must make the adolescent aware that he or she will modify the standards of confidentiality, should it be necessary, in order to protect the adolescent. Suicidal intent is not a secret and families must be involved.

The therapist must deal with the environmental problems of the youth, facilitating re-entry into school, too, if necessary. Teachers and clergy should be called upon as additional supports for youth.

Intervention also must be made with the family. Parents should be helped to deal with their unresolved dependency conflicts and given support so that they can give more to their children. The adolescent should not be singled out as the "sick member" but rather as the member who has alerted everyone to a trouble spot within the family which needs further investigation.

If the family is not amenable to therapy, then therapeutic afternoon programs for troubled adolescents may be advisable to give the youth additional environmental support. Occasionally, an adolescent with recurrent self-destructive behavior who is not compliant with outpatient care may require long-term hospitalization. Long-term hospitalization would offer intensive therapy aimed at changing a maladaptive personality style in a protective setting.

VI

Sadly, all too often the adults in whom suicidal adolescents confide become frightened by a potential suicide and cannot offer the help these adolescents need. This anxiety is aroused in part because these adults have had similar desperate feelings and wish to repress them. Other adults fear they will not be able accurately to assess and ameliorate the situation. These fears evidence the need for further education on the subject of suicide. Health classes dealing with suicide should be established in schools, community centers, and certainly incorporated in all medical and non-medical professional training. Suicide hotlines should be established and community supports for young people be given priority.

The more information on adolescent suicide that is disseminated, the more the public will be able to understand and support their teenagers. This may create some new heroes who are able to recognize the potential attempter and intervene before a tragedy occurs.

REFERENCES

1. Corder, B. F., Shorr, W., & Corder, R. F. A study of social and psychological characteristics of adolescent suicide attempters in an urban, disadvantaged area. *Adolescence*, Spring 1974. *9*(33) 1–6.
2. Curran, B. E. Suicide. *Pediatric Clinics of North America* November 1979 *26*(4) 737–46.
3. Erlich, H. S. Adolescent suicide: maternal longing and cognitive development. *Psychoanalitic Study of the Child* 1978, *33* 261–77.
4. Flinn, D. E., & Leonard, C. V. Prevalence of suicidal ideation and behavior among basic trainees and college students. *Military Medicine*, August 1972, *137*, 317–20.
5. Frederick, C. J. Adolescent suicide. In *Advocacy For Children*, U.S. Department of Health, Education and Welfare, Fall 1978.
6. Golburgh, S. J. (Ed.), *The experience of adolescence*, Cambridge, Mass: 1965.
7. Goldberg, E. L. Depression and suicide ideation in the young adult. *American Journal of Psychiatry*, January 1981, *138*(1), 35–40.
8. Haim, A. *Adolescent suicide*, (A.M.S. Smith, trans.) *International Universities Press*, New York, 1974.
9. Hart, N. A., & Keidel, G. C. The suicidal adolescent. *American Journal of Nursing* January 1979, *79*(1), 80–4.
10. Hersh, S. P. Suicide: Youth's high vulnerability to it/ signs to look for/ how you can help. Summer 1975, *Mental Health 59*(3), 23–5.

11. Hofmann, A. D. Adolescents in distress. Suicide and out-of-control behaviors. *Medical Clinics of North America* November 1975, *459*(6), 1429–37.
12. Jacobs, J. *Adolescent suicide.* New York: Wiley-Interscience 1971.
13. Kenny, T. J., Rohn, R., Sarles, R. M., Reynolds, B. J., & Heald, F. P. Visual-motor problems of adolescents who attempt suicide. *Perceptual and Motor Skills,* April 1979, *48*(2), 599–602.
14. King, M. Evaluation and treatment of suicide-prone youth. *Mental Hygiene,* July 1971, *55*, 344–50.
15. Kreider, D. G., Motto, J. A. Parent-child role reversal and suicidal states in adolescence. *Adolesence,* Fall 1974, *9*(35), 365–70.
16. McAnarney, E. R. Adolescent and young adult suicide in the United States—a reflection of societal unrest? *Adolescence,* Winter 1979, *14*(56), 765–74.
17. _____: Suicidal behavior of children and youth. *Pediatric Clinics of North America,* August 75, *22*(3) 595–604.
18. McIntire, M., & Angle, C. R. (Eds.) *Suicide attempts in children and youth.* New York: Harper & Row, 1980.
19. McKenry, P. C., Tishler, C. L., & Christman, K. L. Adolescent suicide and the classroom teacher. *Journal of School Health* March 1980, *50*(3), 130–2.
20. Otto, U. Suicidal acts by children and adolescents. A follow-up·study. *Acta Psychiatrica Scandinavica,* 1972, (supplement) *233*, 7–123.
21. Pfeffer, C. R. Suicidal behavior of children: a review with implications for research and practice. *American Journal of Psychiatry,* February 1981, *138*(2), 154–9.
22. Richman, J., & Rosenbaum, M. Suicide in children and adolescents. In *Pediatrics,* H. L. Barnett & A. H. Einhorn (Eds.). (15th ed.) New York: Appleton-Century-Crofts, 1972.
23. Rosenkrantz, A. L. A note on adolescent suicide: Incidence, dynamics, and some suggestions for treatment. *Adolescence,* Summer 1978, *13*(50), 209–14.

24. Schecter, M. D., & Sternlof, R. E. Suicide in adolescents. *Postgraduate Medicine,* May 1970, *47* 220–3.
25. Schlebush, L., & Minnaar, G. K. The management of parasuicide in adolescents. *South African Medical Journal* January 19, 1980, *57*(3), 81–4.
26. Shneidman, E. S. Suicide. In *Comprehensive textbook of psychiatry* A. M. Freedman, et al. (Eds.) (Vol. II). Baltimore, Md:, The Williams and Wilkins Co., 1975.
27. Teicher, J. D. Children and adolescents who attempt suicide. *Pediatric Clinic of North America* August 1970, *17*, 687–96.
28. Weissman, M. M. The epidemiology of suicide attempts, 1960 to 1971. *Archives of General Psychiatry,* June 1974, *30*, 737–46.
29. Wenz, F. V. Sociological correlates of alienation among adolescent suicide attempts. *Adolescence,* Spring 1979, *14*(53), 19–30.

Chapter 8

ADOLESCENT SUICIDE:
PREVENTION AND TREATMENT

Rita Wieczorek

Suicide is the voluntary and intentional taking of one's own life. It is a lethal human act that has become the third leading cause of death in adolescents. The suicide of youth is not restricted to any specified age group, geographic area, social class, or cultural background (Wieczorek & Natapoff, 1981). The male teenager, however, is more prone than the female to both attempted and actual suicide completion. It has been estimated that rates of adolescent attempted suicides to completed suicides are approximately 100 to 1 (Heald, 1976). Suicide can happen to anyone, anytime and anyplace. The personality, character, temperament, and emotional stability of the individual person are significant factors in helping suicidal youngsters. Timely prevention is of utmost importance in rescuing adolescents from prematurely ending their lives. Identification of the suicidal adolescent is paramount. Some clues are:

loss of a significant other

recent suicide of a peer or family member

legal difficulty caused by delinquent behavior, drugs, or alcohol abuse

unwanted pregnancy

family stress, either psychological or financial

recent and frequent changes in school, home, or work environments

difficulty in relationships with friends, family, and co-workers

depression and withdrawal

disorientation, disorganization, and isolation

After identification of the teenagers at risk for suicide, the health care worker focuses on lowering their stress, decreasing their isolation from others, and becoming actively involved in solving their problems. The goal is to help the teenager learn to cope with life in a more positive manner.

The health care worker needs to gather some base-line data on the client. The first area assessed is usually related to demographic characteristics. The information gathered in this area includes:

name

age

sex

race

health history (physical and psychological)

religion

current address

permanent address

education (grade level is compared to age)

phone number

living arrangements (family, friends, lover)

Some teenagers may refuse to give this information. This happens more frequently when the youngster seeks help through a hot-line or crisis service. If the client refuses to give specific demographic information, the health care provider should respect the client's decision. In a clinic or other structured health facility teenagers may feel more free to share this information in a face-to-face encounter. It is then easier to establish a sense of trust. On the telephone emotional support seems less personal. When the client is admitted to an inpatient service, this information is not an issue because admission procedures and forms solve the problem.

Reliable statistics on adolescent suicides are hard to obtain with any degree of confidence. Some problems are:

Parents or significant others may attempt to cover up a teenager's attempt or actual suicide because of their own fears and anxieties.

Some persons consider suicide a disgraceful or irreligious act to be "hidden in the closet."

Teenagers or family members may lie and falsify records because of fear of discrimination or fear that they will not receive professional services.

Some reported "accidents" are actual suicide attempts.

Some health care providers will also attempt to "cover up" the facts to "help" the youngster or the family.

Statistical suicide reports related to members of minority groups, sex differences, and religious and cultural background vary. At this point the reports are still conflicting. The safest statement is probably that there is no concrete consistent proof of these differences. The traditional myths associated with adolescent violent behavior are breaking down in today's society.

Most adolescents who attempt or commit suicide have a combination of long-standing problems dating back to earlier childhood. These problems may involve troubled relationships, a lack of academic achievement, or failure in some desired activity related to sports or a job. To these concerns the teenager will also be experiencing the stressful but normal growth and development phenomenon of the age period. Clinical characteristics vary from individual to individual depending on the circumstances surrounding their problems. The suicide hazard is usually due to a recent maturational or situational crisis that has been blown out of proportion. The teenager interprets this recent event as a threat to his/her own personhood. In crisis, some recent traumatic event sets up a tremendous amount of internal turmoil. It is important for the health provider quickly to assess the extent of the crisis' impact on the client's level of functioning. The following questions may serve as a guideline for this information:

Does the youngster exhibit mild, moderate, or severe personality changes?

Is the teenager able to cope with normal daily activities and routines?

Does the crisis cause the youngster to become depressed?

Is the depression severe enough to lead to suicidal thoughts?

Once this is assessed, the health provider focuses on the coping strategies of the youngster in regard to the crisis situation. One must be able to identify quickly how the crisis is being managed. Some teenagers feel so overwhelmed that they need assistance to determine both old and new ways of coping with their intense stress. Mechanisms for coping can either be of a positive or a negative nature. Examples are excessive intake of alcohol, use of drugs, changing jobs, changing schools, seeking support from close friends or family, and concentration on a sport activity. The support system for the troubled youth may be a family member, close peer, or a boyfriend or girlfriend. Teenagers are no different than other age groups who need special support systems to help them in their down periods.

Suicide plans may be laid by the youngster when he or she feels that life is too troublesome to continue. The wish to fight or solve problems no longer exists. Teenagers then want to give up on living. Suicide plans are serious because they can become the route to the final act. It is during this stage that the teenager selects the method to be used for the attempt. The health care provider should assess how quickly the youngster plans to do it and what other arrangements have been thought out surrounding the event such as the date, time, and place. It is also important for the health care provider to know how available the method is to the youngster. A determination of the lethality of the method is made.

A teenager with a past history of accident-proneness and/or prior suicide attempt is a great risk for suicide violence. When the attempt is about to occur the teenager usually becomes completely isolated, disoriented, and extremely hostile to the self. Once the adolescent makes the decision to attempt suicide he or she generally acts on it. In some cases the youngster may notify a close former friend or parent that he/she is thinking about ending his/her life. The notification can be given directly or indirectly. It is often the last cry for help. Not all teenagers engage in this notification process, however.

Why do some teenagers attempt suicide and others not when they experience similar types of problems? The answer is not a simple one but is a complex issue that probably involves a series of individual factors. Besides the stressful events previously mentioned (unwanted pregnancy, prosecution for criminal behavior, recent changes in family membership and roles) psychotic illness can also predispose the teenager to suicidal behavior. Severe depression, bipolar affective disease, and schizophrenia are examples of psychiatric illness. Medical and surgical health problems may also be the precipatory factor in a suicide. This is especially true if the underlying health problem is one that is chronic, long-term in nature, has a fatal prognosis, is physically disfiguring, or renders the teenager a handicapped individual.

Role of the Health Provider

The health provider's role in suicide prevention or intervention is now the focus. It is paramount to provide a supportive first contact for the troubled youngster when the teenager enters the health care system. The adolescent may remain within the community or could be hospitalized. When an identified suicide attempt occurs, hospitalization is usually recommended. The separation that occurs when the teenager is admitted to an inpatient service allows for physical care, observation of behavior, and psychiatric services. Hospitalization is an intense crisis for the teenager and his or her family. Health care providers may have emotional blind spots in treating the youngster because of their own unresolved feelings about suicide. They may also focus on physical problems, thus avoiding the psychological problems of the teenager.

When a youngster seeks help for suicidal thoughts, plans, or behavior, immediate intervention is necessary. The best results probably can be obtained by the use of the appropriate members of the multidisciplinary health team. This may include the following types of specialists: internist, psychiatrist, nurse, social worker, and occupational therapist. Team members are always selected according to the client's special needs. In some instances however, just one psychiatric counselor or therapist may be more effective in treating the client. The team approach does involve time. Regardless of which approach is used, the first thing to decide is how much of the situation is an emergency needing immediate crisis intervention.

When the health providers are involved in a therapeutic relationship with a suicidal adolescent, there are certain general principles that should be adhered to. These are ranked in order of importance.

> Focus first on establishing a relationship that is warm, understanding, personal, and empathic. Most suicidal teenagers are isolated and withdrawn from others. They are absolutely starving for a relationship with a caring human being. The health care provider should be attentive, supportive, and a good listener.
> Next it is important to build a sense of trust. This is something that occurs over time as the relationship is established. Being an accepting person will help the client regain a feeling of self-worth. In building a sense of trust, the health care provider must be honest. The parameters of the relationship should be structured, mutual rules for the relationship established, a contract set up, and

confidentiality respected. The troubled youth should feel safe discussing his/her problems and thoughts. The health provider has to be able to size up each session or meeting. Confrontation techniques are better not used in the first few visits. After trust has been established, the teenager can better tolerate criticism and differences of opinion. Anger and hostility are going to be displayed. Manipulation may be tried. Constant assurance is usually necessary. Both the therapist and the client should be frank about their likes and dislikes.

Family and close friends of the suicidal teenager should be included in the therapy sessions as deemed appropriate. Many suicidal teenagers are part of a disturbed environment. Crisis intervention should be family-centered if at all possible. Better understanding of each other's needs is thus obtained.

The health providers are now ready to focus on solving the current suicidal hazard or crisis. It is necessary for the teenager to have some feeling of self-worth before he or she can begin to work on solving his/her problems. Health personnel can be helpful to the troubled youth by decreasing the threat (to the teenager). It is important for the adolescent to understand the problems realistically. When a youngster is faced with multiple problems, priorities should be set and goals established. Each problem is best conquered by working on it individually so it can be set in proportion to other things.

Health providers should be able to determine specific needs of the client based on their in-

terpretation of the data. Several resources that may be helpful in individual situations are:
temporary foster care
use of psychiatric medications
providing for self-protection of the client from himself or herself.
enlisting the help of other professionals and family members to relieve some of the stress on the teenager
using crisis intervention resources in the community for both psychological and physical needs.

The goal of the suicidal intervention is to help the client cope with normal activities, rejoin social structures, handle stress in a healthy manner, become oriented to the environment and organized enough to meet their own needs. The health provider should be prepared for periods of successes and setbacks. The road to good mental health may be a rocky one but it is one worth working toward. The health providers working with adolescents should enjoy these young people. They must have a strong theoretical base in normal growth and development of the age group. It is important to realize that adolescence spans many years and many stresses occur during this time period.

REFERENCES

Heald, F.P. Morbidity and mortality. In J.R. Gallagher et al. *Medical Care of the Adolescent*. (3rd ed.). New York: Appleton-Century-Crofts, 1976.

Wieczorek, R.R., & Natapoff, J.N. *A conceptual approach to the nursing of children*. Philadelphia: J.B. Lippincott Co., 1981.

Chapter 9

SUICIDAL IDEATION IN TERMINALLY ILL PATIENTS AND THEIR FAMILIES

William S. Liss-Levinson

In bringing together two subjects which society has traditionally viewed as taboo—suicide and terminal illness—the author hopes to explore a variety of issues that health and human service professionals need to confront when dealing with terminally ill persons and their family members. The focus will be on suicidal ideation as it is an expressed reaction to the illness.

I. INCIDENCE OF SUICIDAL IDEATION AMONG THE TERMINALLY ILL

The issue of the actual incidence of suicidal ideation among the terminally ill is one which has yet to be addressed by researchers both in suicidology and thanatology. We do know that there is even a lack of extensive research on actual suicidal behavior among this population. Danto (in

Goldberg et al., 1973) and Cantor (1978) both consider the incidence of suicidal behavior among the terminally ill to be rare. Suicidal ideation, however, is very difficult to assess. First, many patients and/or their family members are very reluctant to share these thoughts with others, be they family, friends, or professionals. Patients may have fears of being a "bad" person for having such thoughts. Often people are concerned that they will be letting their family or physician down if they "give up hope," as well as perhaps even potentially hasten their death by their emotional state. In addition, many health and human service professionals are themselves reluctant to explore the whole issue of suicide with their patients. They may, therefore, not question the patient and/or family, or perhaps not follow through on certain cues or hints regarding the suicidal ideation. Such professionals would thus be apt to report a very low incidence of this ideation, in fact more reflective of their own inability to confront the issue.

The author, in his work over the past 4 years with over 500 terminally ill patients and their family members, has only observed one completed suicide and one suicide attempt among these persons. However, probably from 40 to 50 percent of the patients have at one time considered suicide as an alternative to their current existence. This is not to say that each of these persons articulated this ideation directly, e.g., "I've been thinking about killing myself." Rather, they have in various direct and indirect ways expressed the idea that they would be better off dead, or that if they took their own life their suffering would end, or something similar. Family members, to a much lesser extent, also express such ideation. In perhaps 5 to 10 percent of the cases I have seen, family members would express, again in direct and in indirect ways, some suicidal thought.

The ensuing sections will address: major causal factors for the ideation as expressed by the patient and the family member; assessment of suicide lethality; and therapeutic intervention issues.

II. CAUSAL FACTORS: THE PATIENT

Pain

Perhaps the single most causal factor for suicidal ideation as expressed by a terminally ill patient is *pain*. It is important here to distinguish between *current, experienced pain*, and *projected future pain*. In reacting to current pain, the patient is generally experiencing pain that is poorly managed and/or poorly tolerated, both from pharmacologic and psychologic perspectives. Regarding projected pain, the patient is saying, "I can deal with my present illness, and impending death, *but* if there will be pain/an increase in my current pain in the future, then I'd rather kill myself/be dead." This is particularly common with people who have advanced cancer, and often assume, frequently erroneously, that they will, by the disease's definition, be subject to intense and uncontrollable pain at some future time. In both these situations, actively hastening death is seen as a means of achieving ultimate relief from the pain.

The Patient as a "Burden"

Another factor raised by patients is the notion of being a *burden* to family members. While sometimes the patient is referring to being an emotional burden, more often they perceive themselves as a physical and/or financial burden. This again, as in the case of pain, may be expressed in terms of their current status, or projected future status.

On perhaps a more existential level, some patients feel

that they are a *burden to themselves.* That is, continuing to live in a decreasingly functional state is physically burdensome to them.

In these situations, the patient views suicide as the "best" way to facilitate a rapid alleviation of the burdensome state by directly eliminating the burden, i.e. themselves.

Emotional Stresses and Existential Issues

Patients who feel overwhelmed by *anxiety* about their death, or anxiety about the medical interventions they are subjected to, may also consider suicide as an alternative. More often, the patient who is severely *depressed* and *despondent*, feeling a complete loss of hope, is likely to contemplate suicide. For many people, the process of dying represents both a loss of dignity and control (Cantor, 1978). Interactions with numerous health care institutions and professionals often rob people of their right to make decisions about their lives. Despite advances in the area of patients' rights, the average person dying in this country will be probed, poked, scanned, and stuck by a variety of persons whose names and faces become blurs. If an individual feels that he/she has been deprived of the ability to be master of his/her life, as well as if he/she has always placed a high value on this self-control, the sense of despondency is intensified. Patients often talk about feeling they are no longer the same person they used to be or that it is as if they have already died. The prospect of suicide can thus be seen as the sole way for the person to (regain) gain control over his/her life by controlling the time and circumstances of death.

Attention-Seeking Behavior

Perhaps one of the most difficult situations to assess is when the expressions of the suicidal ideation seem to be reflective of what is commonly referred to as "attention-seeking behavior." Often there is some indication that the patient is expressing these ideas primarily as a means of manipulating the family and/or professionals to attend to them and their needs. The reader who is familiar with health care institutions can easily see how such suicidal ideation would mobilize a concerted effort on the part of all staff to attend to the patient and to monitor the patient more frequently than is usual. Staff may thus check in on the patient more often, talk at greater length, etc. The family may visit more often and express their love and concern more directly. Additional health care professionals, such as psychiatric nurses, social workers, psychologists, or psychiatrists may suddenly be assigned to evaluate and treat the patient.

So called "attention-seeking behavior" should be an indication of a number of things. First and foremost, we need to determine if in fact the patient really has some needs that are not being adequately addressed by the staff or family. Second, even if there are no glaring needs being neglected, this behavior is an indication that something more is needed or desired by the patient than is being received. Finally, we must not fall into the trap of labelling such behaviors as "bad" or inappropriate. Such labelling usually leads to health care professionals responding punitively to the patient and decreasing the quantity and quality of their contact with the person.

III. CAUSAL FACTORS: THE FAMILY

While the incidence of suicidal ideation appears to be rather low among the family members of terminally ill persons, health care and human service professionals should be aware of the major factor that seems to cause these thoughts.

Inability to Cope with the Loss

The basic underlying causal factor seems to be the feeling that the family member will not be able to cope with the death of the patient. This may be articulated in a variety of ways. A family member may say "I don't want to live without him." Here, the projected psychic pain and grief over the loss is so severe that life would no longer be meaningful. Another response is when the person says, "Her loss will be too painful for me to handle, even though I would like to be able to cope." In this case, the family member is not always fully aware of what this fear of not being able to cope involves. When pursued further by the skilled clinician, many such people are in fact fearful of becoming so distraught and depressed that they would have a "nervous breakdown" and eventually commit suicide from the combination of depression and loss of meaning and control.

It is often very difficult for family members to admit to their suicidal ideations. The primary focus at this time is on the dying person, the medical condition, emotional reactions, etc. Many times, family members' feelings can be overlooked because of the intense focus on the patient. This situation may be reinforced if the health or human service professional is apt to avoid dealing with suicide to begin with. Also family members expressing such suicidal ideation often generate a great deal of guilt. They may feel that they are selfish or egocentric if they are worried about themselves, when they're not suffering or dying. They may also find that if they do express these feelings others will inflict guilt upon them for precisely those reasons.

IV. ASSESSMENT OF SUICIDE LETHALITY

Any expression of suicidal ideation, by either a terminally ill person or the family, must be taken seriously and serve as an impetus for an immediate and complete assessment of the actual suicide risk. The following is a brief overview of the issues that need to be explored in order to assess the actual suicide potential posed.

History

A thorough history of the individual should be taken, emphasizing the nature of previous life stresses and the person's ability to cope with these events (including positive life stresses such as marriage and childbirth). Certainly, the clinician should be aware of any previous illness and the individual's response to them. It is important to determine if there is a history of emotional "disturbances," "break-downs," violent behavior (self or other-directed), suicidal ideation, and, most obviously, suicide attempts. An analysis of the individual's support systems, be they family or friends, is also essential. Finally, it will be helpful if it can be determined how much perceived self-control the person has at the present time (as well as what this individual has generally felt about the ability to control impulses).

Detail of Plans and Lethality of Method

It is important to discuss with the person whether he/she has given much thought to suicide, and specifically to the method to be utilized. The method must be fully explored both regarding the details of the plan as well as the lethality and availability of the method to the individual. For example, people who indicate that they would "take some pills," without appearing to have considered what pills, how many pills, and where and how they would obtain them, may be at very low risk for actual suicide attempts. On the other hand, an individual who talks in terms of using a gun or a rifle (a highly "successful" method) and owns both gun or rifle and ammunition, is clearly at greater risk. It is critical in these circumstances that the health care or human services professional not be afraid to "push" the individual and the issue in order to understand fully the person's plans. (Obviously this is not to suggest that excessive questioning of the individual in the absence of a good trust relationship is called for).

Circumstances

Suicidal thoughts are often expressed in terms of the circumstances under which the person would consider taking his/her life. For example, a patient might say, "I'd kill myself if I could no longer walk or control my bladder or bowels, etc." It might also be expressed as, "If the pain gets so bad that . . . " or, "If I ever get to be a burden to my family where they need to put me in a nursing home, etc." Certainly it is crucial to explore if this person targets a particular date or event in the future after which he/she would commit suicide, such as birthdays, religious holidays, anniversaries, etc.

Other Indicators

Sometimes a patient or a family member who is contemplating suicide gives "clues" to this ideation. For example, the person who suddenly decides to write and/or finalize a will, or to increase insurance coverage, may be indicating to us that the house is being put in order prior to death. An unexpected discussion of which household items are designated for individual family members upon the person's death may also be a sign of undisclosed suicidal ideation. Finally, as was mentioned in the preceding section, references to forthcoming events or dates as the "last" one the person expects to celebrate may also be an indicator that should be pursued.

Therapeutic Intervention Issues[1]

As was previously indicated, few terminally ill persons or their family members are actually at a higher than average risk for suicide. The focus of therapeutic intervention, therefore, must be to help the individual to understand his/her ideation and thus to begin to deal effectively with those causal or contributing factors that have led to these thoughts.

The causal factors have been discussed in Section II and III. This section will discuss those issues that the health and human services professional will need to address in the course of interventions with terminally ill persons or their family members. While many of the issues will be the same for both patient and family member, there are some unique factors that should be addressed in interventions with family members. For purposes of clarity, these are discussed at the end of this section.

---

[1]This discussion is by no means to be exhaustive of the therapeutic intervention strategies, approaches, and techniques that may be employed. The reader will do well to examine works such as Kiev (1977) or Schneidman (1976), in addition to this chapter, for more complete analyses and interventions.

Normalcy

The therapist may first need to convey to the individual that suicidal ideation is well within the range of "normal" behavior for persons undergoing such severe stress. The greatest fear that people seem to have is that their ideation is an indication of their being "crazy." Reassurance that other people in their situation have similar thoughts can ease the psychic burden the individual is carrying. The clinician might also do well to consider the possibility, if deemed appropriate, of introducing the individual to another patient or family member who also expressed such thoughts and successfully dealt with the issues.

Distinction between Ideation and Behavior

The second major issue that sould be addressed is the distinction between *thinking* about suicide and *acting* upon these thoughts. While most of us don't normally confuse these two processes, the fear generated by ideation which is considered anything from "bad" to morally reprehensible negates the usual awareness we have of this distinction. People need to be reassured that they are still in control of themselves, and able to monitor and control their thoughts, no matter how distrubing or "wrong" these thoughts may seem.

Guilt

Even when the clinician addresses the two preceding issues, many persons still cannot accept the basic fact that they allowed themselves to entertain thoughts about ending their lives. It is not uncommon for people who have strong religious beliefs that include prohibitions against suicide to feel that they have sinned, are bad, and are no longer loved by God. Even those who do not go to this extreme in their guilt may feel that these thoughts are an indication of moral weakness. Again, reassurance of both the normalcy of these thoughts, even among people with strong religious beliefs, is important. The clinician should also consider intervention by the person's clergy, provided that this pastor does not subscribe to the "sin" theory of suicidal ideations.

Active Therapeutic Intervention Focus

While the initial thrust of the intervention may be to dispel some of the negative, self-destructive myths people may have, nonetheless, the person needs to know that there is a serious issue that must be addressed. The clinician should explore with the individual the factors that have contributed to the suicidal ideation. The factors will be specific to the individual, but generally the clinician will need to help the person reduce the depression or anxiety experienced. (It should be clear, however, that this goal must be one that is shared by the person, i.e., that he/she *wants* to be less depressed or anxious.) Certainly if pain is the major causal factor, the clinician may need to intervene with the health care team to effect better pain and symptom control. Assurances that future, potential pain will be handled so that the patient need not suffer will be critical. It is important to remember that if we are to promise an individual a pain-free existence in the present or in the future, we had better be prepared to back this up with palliative intervention when needed.

It has been this author's experience that ongoing supportive counseling regarding the various general issues facing the person will register impact on suicidal ideation, and thus is an important adjunct to any crisis intervention approach.

Clearly there may be persons for whom a pharmacologic approach is necessary, be it tranquilizers or antidepressants. It is very important to weigh the possible benefits of these agents against the possible negative implications. For one, medicating a patient with these drugs in effect increases the availability of a method of suicide, i.e., overdosing on the medication. Furthermore, for the person who is already grappling with the loss of control a terminal illness presents, the "need" for medication may be perceived as a further sign of their inability to control themselves, their emotions, and their lives. If it is deemed appropriate to use such agents, it should be discussed openly with the person so that he/she feels confident that the drugs are being used in their own best interest, to *assist them* to better cope with their stresses.

It cannot be overemphasized that there may be a need for intervention in the area of finances and other "concrete" social services. Often the source of anxiety and depression may be fears regarding reimbursement for health care, daily living expenses, or funeral and burial costs. The clinician may not be equipped to refer the individual to someone who can address these various issues quickly.

As was previously mentioned, pastoral counseling and support can be an adjunct to the professional therapist's interventions. Again, caution must be exercised in selecting a clergyperson (or in utilizing the person's own clergy) for this task. It is important to ascertain that such clergy will be consistent in approach with the attitude and approaches of the clinician.

Finally, working with the person in a vacuum without involvement of other family members or significant others in the person's life is not to be recommended. The issues that will be raised in the therapeutic interventions almost certainly will have an impact on other persons and they too should be involved when deemed appropriate.

Special Issues for Intervention with Family Members

For the family members of a terminally ill person, many of their fears that contribute to the suicidal ideation relate to concerns about their ability to cope with the death of their loved one. They need reassurance that while the loss may be extremely painful, they can and will be able to cope with it. Helping people to deal with their anticipatory grief may thus be critical at this point.

On a very pragmatic level, family members may need training in certain life skills (e.g., cooking, budgeting, etc.) as a way to assure them that they will be able effectively to survive the death. Certainly for the person who fears never again being able to develop any social or intimate relationships, training in "basic social and interpersonal skills" would be beneficial. The year following the death of a loved one can be a critical one for the bereaved survivors, both from a physical and emotional health standpoint. The individual should be appraised of the availability of the clinician or other clinicians for bereavement counseling should that be needed and desired.

V. MORAL AND LEGAL ISSUES

While it is beyond the scope of this discussion to address the myriad moral and legal implications of suicide as an alternative for the terminally ill, the health and human service professional needs to be aware of the basic issues. Groups such as the New York City-based *Concern for Dying* have devoted entire conferences to the various moral and legal questions that may confront the professional grappling with this situation. Certainly any professional dealing with this population should have a basic knowledge of the state's laws that apply to such situations, both regarding the person who attempts or commits suicide, as well as regarding the health or human service professional's responsibility in these cases. An awareness of one's own attitudes and feelings regardng suicide, in general, and as an alternative for the terminally ill, would also be helpful, particularly as they relate to one's therapeutic interventions.

SUMMARY

This chapter has given an overview of suicidal ideation in terminally ill persons and their family members. While it is by no means an exhaustive review of the issues involved, it should provide the reader with a foundation upon which further investigations can be based.

As our society attains newer levels of technological and medical sophistication we will have more "sick" people living for longer periods of time until they are terminally ill, and perhaps even living longer in the "terminal" state than before. We must be prepared to face the awesome responsibility of responding to their medical, psychosocial, spiritual, and financial needs. Suicidal ideation and its concomitant psychological implications represent one such area of need that we will have to confront openly and honestly, from a position of both competence and caring.

REFERENCES

Cantor R. C. *And a time to live: Toward emotional well-being during the crisis of cancer.* New York: Harper & Row, Inc., 1978

Danto, B. The cancer patient and suicide. In I. Goldberg, S. Malitz, & A. Kutscher, (Eds.). *Psychopharmacologic agents for the terminally ill and bereaved.* New York: Foundation of Thanatology, 1973.

Kiev, A. *The suicidal patient: Recognition and management.* Chicago: Nelson-Hall, Inc. 1977.

Schneidman, E. (Ed.) *Suicidology: Contemporary developments.* New York: Grune & Stratton, 1976.

Part II

INTERVENTION WITH
BEREAVED SURVIVORS
OF SUICIDE

INTRODUCTION

Section II deals with the "after" of suicide, the impact of the suicide on the bereaved families, and the role of mental health practitioners in the grief process. The particular concern of these authors is the special nature of bereavement after suicide as distinct from other forms of death. Suicide will have a differential impact on survivors, depending on whether it was committed by a child, a parent, or a grandparent. In all cases, the entire family is involved.

Chapter 10, *Family Factors in Bereavement Following a Death by Suicide*, focuses on the family as a whole. The bereaved family has two alternatives: to deal with the loss appropriately—a positive outcome; or not to deal with it appropriately—a negative outcome—which can lead to dissension and mental illness. The case of the mother who did not inform her children of their father's suicide led to months of intensive therapy. Therapy is a delicate process and it may be extended by the funeral director and family counselor. It is most effective when it is given close to the crisis. The author proposes a change in society's attitude toward the suicide. A greater acceptance by society will encourage troubled people to seek help.

Chapter 11, *Children's Reactions to a Suicide in the Family and their Implications for Treatment*, reviews studies of the impact of parental suicide on child survivors and their subsequent suicidal behavior. Prior to intervention, the therapist needs to consider the age of the child, for the suicide will make a differential impact depending upon the child's developmental stage. The circumstances of the suicide and how and when the child finds out are also significant variables. In the assessment procedure, the therapist screens the family members, inquires about the child's and parent's personal life prior to the suicide, and the behavior and mood of the child. In treatment, the therapist deals with the child's guilt, fears of abandonment, and of losing control. The therapist encourages honest communication in the family, and using the family members to help the child to cope with the loss.

Chapter 12, *Crisis: Psychological First Aid for Recovery and Growth*, describes at length the suicide of a fourteen-year-old boy who shot himself with his father's gun. The parents' guilt was enormous; the therapist's interventions and her care and deep involvement throughout the long process was very helpful to the family. The author advocates that suicide not be judged as a sin which is hushed, denied, and avoided, and that all efforts be expended to prevent suicide among those who survive. In this chapter, the reader is privy to a therapist at work.

Chapter 13, *A Mother's Personal Experience in the Loss of a Son through Suicide*, describes the pain, struggle, conflict, renewal, and working through of grief, anger, and devastation that the family, and particularly the mother experienced when the son committed suicide. The description of the process is vivid and heart-rending. A central theme keeps reappearing—the need to face up to the tragedy no matter how painful. "I needed to go through the pain to get beyond it." The openness and honesty of the author encouraged the audience to ask questions which she answered with frankness. She also describes her work as director of a counseling center for bereaved families and potential suicides, its philosophy and approach deeply influenced by her grief experience.

Chapter 14, *First-Line Help Following a Funeral*, describes suicide as a cruel death that does not obviate the necessity of holding a funeral. Survivors may want to hold it quickly to avoid the shame, and may even arrange a private funeral. Hiding the fact is a mistake that the family makes, for friends can lend supporting love in these moments of anguish. The funeral is a rite of separation. In this way the process of denial can be transformed to the acceptance of reality. The goals in ministering to the family of the suicide are similar to those in helping all who face bereavement. Clergy and care givers can bring to the fore their best self which is not prejudicial nor judgmental of the actions of the deceased or the survivors. They should encourage "grief work"—talking about the event, ventilating reactions, reviewing memories of the deceased. If there are any doubts to the care giver as to the bereaved's emotional health, professional help should be obtained.

Chapter 15, *Intervention by the Pastoral Counselor with Survivors of a Suicide*, suggests that in the counseling process work, more than ventilation is needed. The counselor should try to alleviate in the mourner self-accusations regarding his/her role in the suicide. The mourners experience special pain after a suicide of a family member. Pastoral Bereavement Counseling relies on the principles of intervention such as empathy, support, endurance, and acceptance, and is limited and focused in order to prevent excessive dependency on the counselor. From a religious point of view, the bereaved have a special religious cry against God. The normal anger against God cannot be faced as clearly in the case of suicide. The pastoral counselor strives to restore the basic meaning of life and worthiness of struggle, to replace the sense of tragedy and waste.

Chapter 10

FAMILY FACTORS IN BEREAVEMENT
FOLLOWING A DEATH BY SUICIDE

Joseph Richman

This chapter is concerned with the two basic alternatives faced by the surviving family members following a
death by suicide: 1) There may be a positive outcome when
the family is able to deal with the death appropriately,
where the loss may actually draw everyone closer into a
cohesive community of loving helpers and lead to further
growth and improved adjustment in the survivors; or 2)
There may be a negative outcome when the situation is
not dealt with directly or appropriately. There the suicide
may lead to increased dissension, discord and mental illness, physical illness, and/or suicide in the individual members. The period immediately following a suicide is a particularly crucial time, during which the future fate, and
even the very lives of some survivors, may be determined.

The tendencies toward secrecy and denial in families
where a suicide has occurred may present formidable stum-

bling blocks that can prevent a constructive resolution of the tragedy. Freud (1957) made the point that a successful process of mourning requires an acknowledgement of the reality of the loss. When this mourning process is successful there is an expansion and enlargement of the self, which leads to further growth and self-fulfillment. However, when the fact of suicide is kept concealed, and the dark clouds of secrecy and avoidance hang over the family, then the reality is not acknowledged. The effects of this can be very destructive. Cain and Fast (1966) have written eloquently about the legacy of mental illness and further suicides that are subsequently inherited. The family's secretiveness is quite understandable because of the attitudes of Western society. These contribute in a very central manner to the family's problems of guilt and shame, fear of being blamed, and the entire atmosphere of social and private stigma that surrounds a suicide.

Nevertheless, in my experience the survivors are not, in actuality, permanently rejected, realistically hurt, nor objectively harmed by the stigma of a suicide in the family, and they are well rid of those few fair-weather friends who do turn away.

Warmth, maturity, and openness are characteristic of those who have transcended such losses. Elnora (Betsy) Ross was determined to face the personal suffering that followed the suicide of her husband. She founded *Ray of Hope*, a self-help group for those who have undergone a similar loss. Their slogan *Turn a Grief Process into a Growth Process* tells Mrs. Ross's story. Iris Bolton is another who has helped hundreds of others to grieve and find eventual consolation, following the suicide of her young son. Had these courageous people decided to deny, conceal, and dissemble, they could not have made such contributions. Fortunately, they are but a small sample of those who have responded to the tragedy of a suicide by becoming motivated both to help others and to fulfill their own personal destinies. Such positive reactions are predicated upon an acknowledgement of the suicide and the going through of the inevitably painful but necessary grieving process.

However, the therapy or counseling of a family which has been overcome by the turmoil that follows a suicide may be a delicate process, requiring much sensitivity and empathy. An example is that of one mother who had not told her four children that their father committed suicide 3 years before. They believed, at least consciously, that he had died of a heart attack. The changes in their behavior, however, may have reflected a different covert awareness. The oldest daughter became addicted to drugs, the oldest son became suicidal himself, and the two youngest children exhibited a variety of academic and social disturbances. They finally entered psychotherapy, but the mother was not immediately able to tell her children the true state of affairs. It took 5 months of individual therapy with the mother and family therapy for all before she was finally able to confide the truth to her children, and then enter into a more genuine pattern of communication and interaction.

Such difficulties could have been considerably diminished, and even avoided entirely, had some intervention taken place 3 years earlier, immediately after the husband's death. How is that to be accomplished, and by whom? One possibility is the funeral director, a very special kind. Right after a death, a funeral director with the skills and training of a family counselor or else with the collaboration of a family counselor at the funeral home, can be most helpful and perhaps save the lives of survivors.

An analogy can be drawn with what occurs in treatment, where the turmoil of extreme feelings can be expressed and directed into nondestructive and adaptive channels. In my family counseling with suicidal persons, I have found that a family quarrel during therapy is not only therapeutic; it is necessary if progress is to occur. Similarly, such emotional arousal can be turned to advantage at the time funeral arrangements are being made, in order to help bring about a proper funeral and the beginning of a process of mourning and bereavement.

The funeral director and family counselor who are between them trained in family work, suicide prevention, and an understanding of bereavement, first permit and encourage the fullest expresson of such intense feelings and resentments as far as possible, urging everyone to air their views, while maintaining control over the situation. They then intervene, empathically recognizing that such feelings are to be expected when someone dies, especially when the death is due to suicide, and they are glad that the family members are able to express themselves so freely. However, they must not let their feelings overcome their better judgment. It is now their job to prepare for the funeral in the best way possible. The funeral director and family counselor then settle down to work, to help the family members make the necessary arrangements.

In the final phase of the funeral arrangements, they ask the family once again to express their thoughts and feelings about the death and about the deceased, what they all can do to help each other deal with what happened, and to grow from it. In this manner, the funeral director, as a family counselor, may help initiate the grief process that is so necessary, and prevent untold misery in the future.

As can be seen, a major consideration in a therapeutic intervention is timing. The best intervention occurs closest to the situation. This is true of all emergencies, not only death, and of all deaths, not only suicides. Any death can be considered a potential crisis situation for the survivors, calling for crisis intervention. Since death marks the beginning of a grief process among the loved ones in the family and social network, a potential disturbance in bereaved individuals can often be identified immediately. This next section will discuss the indications of a disruption in the mourning process *in the family*. These apply to bereavement in general, not only when the loss is due to suicide.

There are four major danger signs in the family which signal that such a grief process is not taking place or is meeting with difficulties. They include the following:

1. An inability of the family network to mourn, with a specific refusal to allow the person most at risk to go through the grief process. For example, the family members may become excessively upset or angry should he/she openly cry and grieve. Sometimes the relatives will insist that the person most affected move away from the home or location where they lived with the deceased, and to go on a pleasure trip immediately.

A major point is that these family members have themselves not completed the work of mourning old past losses, as Dorpat (1973) pointed out. As a result, the suicidal person and the family have remained particularly vulnerable to loss and separation. This foundation of old unresolved grief work makes the problem of mourning in the present that much more serious, intense, insidious, and cumulative.

2. A turning away from the most bereaved person by the rest of the family system. The most frequent reactions are distancing or becoming unavailable to the grieving one; and an extrusion of the bereaved from the family system.

An example was an eighteen year-old man whose mother died. A few months later his siser married and left home. This was a double loss, for her brother had established a very congenial relationship with this sister's fiancé. Meanwhile, his father took a second job so that he was away both day and night. It was in this context, not at the loss of the mother alone, that the son became suicidal.

3. A role hiatus or gap in the family system, with no one to assume the functions formerly performed by the deceased. The family is left with an incomplete or damaged structure. Sometimes the gap is deliberately maintained by the family to avoid acknowledging the reality of the loss. Sometimes the gap symbolizes the living presence of unfinished business which has to be resolved.

4. A displacement of unfinished conflicts with the deceased upon another member of the family. In several patients who become suicidal following the loss of a loved one, the conflicts that members of the family system are undergoing with the deceased at the time of the death are transferred to the suicidal bereaved.

For example, one man had engaged in violent physical altercations with his wife. Several times she was severely bruised, and their son feared that she would die. Actually, she did die, but from natural causes. After her death, the father and son became involved in violent disagreements, which while stopping short of physical violence, were of frightening intensity. The father began to fear the son would kill him. At one point the son actually picked up a knife during an argument but did not use it. The next day he made a suicide attempt.

Our clinical material indicated that in such examples as the above an identification with the deceased takes place by the potentially suicidal person. In addition, this bereaved is also identified with the deceased by the family, and the two identifications are inextricably intertwined and reinforce each other. Especially when the deceased has committed suicide, these identifications may impel the bereaved to repeat the suicide, both to rejoin the deceased and also to meet the expectations of everyone around him. It is apparent, therefore, that the individual factor is not to be ignored, but it must be placed in the family and social context.

Discussion and Conclusions

The difficulties following a death, especially one by suicide, involve the entire family, not only one individual. It follows that in order to foster optimal adjustment and mental health for survivors, it is desirable to involve the entire family, to help resolve the barriers to proper mourning. By working with the family it is possible to wake up the dormant healing, helping, and growth-inducing forces (Richman, 1979). The entire family can then become a self-help group. The therapist or counselor is especially fortunate should there be family members who can tolerate genuine mourning, who can be honest yet accepting about the fact of suicide, and who can encourage those in greatest need to accept professional help when that is called for.

However, for such developments to occur with greater frequency, a change in the attitude of society may be required, in the direction of removing or at least reducing the aura of stigma, guilt and blame that surround so many suicides. It is then that we shall find suicide prevention measures becoming truly effective. After all, there was a time when cancer, too, was surrounded with a greater aura of shame and concealment than is now the case. Care was exercised never to tell the ill person of the nature of the illness. Today, there is a relatively greater openness and decreased sense of stigma. Many positive developments have followed. For example, people can now more easily be taught the principles of self-examination for cancer, which has probably helped save thousands of lives.

I suggest that the same kind of self-examination for suicide can take place, and that this development will also help save many despairing persons. One problem is that the potentially suicidal person is not always aware or sufficiently free to undergo such a self-examination. However, loved ones in the family and the social network of friends, colleagues, and fellow workers may be. Without the socially reinforced barriers of secrecy and stigma, these caring ones can be freer to note signs of depression, withdrawal, and direct or implicit suicidal communications. They can be especially concerned about the implications of these signs when there has been a recent loss through separation, divorce, or death, or a recent failure in work or school. Self-examination, like self-help for suicide, is a shared and family action.

There are many organizations and social movements which help sustain life. Among these, paradoxically, we might include those that espouse death. There is a growing movement to advocate suicide and to encourage people to kill themselves. *Exit* in Great Britain is one such group, and there are similar ones in the United States. I believe that there is a value to such activities, and that a constructive development may emerge from these advocates of self-destruction. If suicide is considered a matter of personal choice, of the same order of openness as other major individual decisions, then the sense of shame and stigma are removed. Once that occurs, many more people might feel freer to seek and accept help for their suicidal urges. Most such persons feel trapped and in need of help, which they would be more likely to accept were suicide to be discussed openly and socially accepted. Bereavement may thus become more acceptable when a loved one has died through suicide. In a socially accepted setting the survivors can more easily be helped to realize that the deceased person can be grieved for, and this will be followed by a resumption of living.

Thus the advocates of suicide may ultimately be preventing suicide by giving individuals a choice. Their emphasis has been upon *Choosing Suicide* and *The Right to Die*, but the other side of these coins are *Choosing Life*, and *The Right to Live*. The suicidal person would, on the whole, choose life if offered a genuine free choice, including the availability of loving and caring support systems, the opportunity genuinely to mourn, and to pass through the symbolic death and rebirth cycle, which, like sleeping and waking, appears to be part of the essential nature and rhythm of life.

REFERENCES

Cain, A., & Fast, I., Children's disturbed reactions to parent suicide. *American Journal of Orthopsychiatry*, 1966, *36*, 873–880.

Dorpat, T.L., Suicide, loss and mourning. *Life-Threatening Behavior*, 1973, *3*, 213–224.

Freud, S., *Mourning and melancholia*. Standard Edition, (J. Strachey, Ed. and trans.) (Vol. XIV). London: Hogarth, 1957.

Richman, J., The family therapy of attempted suicide. *Family Process*, 1979, *18*, 131—142.

Roman J. *Exit House*. New York: Seaview Books, 1980.

Chapter 11

CHILDREN'S REACTIONS TO A SUICIDE IN THE FAMILY AND THE IMPLICATIONS FOR TREATMENT

Arthur M. Small and *Andrea Diane Small*

Although the importance is great, relatively little attention has been focused on the child as a survivor of a suicide in the family. Each year, approximately 28,000 (*World Almanac*, 1978) Americans commit suicide. Many experts feel this figure is too low and the actual number is closer to 50,000. Even if only one in four victims leaves behind a child, we can estimate that between 7,000 and 12,000 children are added to the survivor-victim population class each year. Since this problem has been an ongoing one for many years, we can reasonably assume there are at least 350,000 to 600,000 children and adults who lost a parent through a suicide while still a child.

During the past 15 years there has been an increasing interest in the study of suicide in the psychiatric and psychological literature. This has resulted in several excellent papers on the recognition of suicidal potential (Pfeffer et al., 1980), the establishment of hotlines and suicide prevention centers, and the treatment of suicidal patients (Wekstein, 1979). However, the acute and long-term treatment of survivors of a suicide, especially with respect to children survivors, has not been given the emphasis it deserves.

Childhood bereavement resulting from parental separation or natural death has been extensively studied by Freud (1959), Deutsch (1937), Klein (1978), and Bowlby (1960). The importance that they attributed to the early parent-child relationship has given rise to the assumption that the rupture of this relationship by death or desertion seriously impedes the emotional development of the child. Sociologists (Volkart & Michael, 1957) point out that such a loss is likely to be more traumatic today in our limited nuclear families than was formerly the case when the traditional extended family was the rule. Death disrupts an ongoing social order. The bereaved child must face not only a personal loss, but also a disruptive vacancy in his or her social order. Bereavement differs, however, from other ruptures—such as desertion, divorce, or separation—since death is fundamentally more mysterious, as well as completely irreversible (Markusen & Fulton, 1971).

The dynamics of the grief process in children will not be discussed here as they have been extensively written on by Bowlby (1961), Kübler-Ross (1969), and others (Kliman, 1968; Lopez & Kliman, 1979), and have also been a topic of several conferences on bereavement and grief (Linzer, 1977). Suffice it to say at this point that the grieving process following a suicide probably occurs in a manner similar to the process following a non-suicidal death, but with additional problems.

The literature is replete with studies showing that children who come from broken homes, either by divorce or death (Bendiksen & Fulton, 1975), are significantly more likely to have committed some offense against the law than are persons from intact homes. This prognosis also holds true for depression (Brown, et al., 1977; Roy, 1981) and other behavioral disorders. Are there any characteristics peculiar to children who survive a suicide? Cain and Fast (1966) reported on 45 children ages four–fourteen who survived a parental suicide and were referred for psychiatric evaluation and/or treatment because of disturbed behavior. Cases were seen from within a few days to more than 10 years after the parent's suicide. In the sample were 32 boys and 13 girls. The mean period between the parent suicide and psychiatric referral was slightly over 4 years. The symptom pictures of the children covered a broad spectrum, including psychosomatic disorders, obesity, running away, delinquency, fetishism, and encopresis along with characterological problems, classical neurotic disorders, and psychotic conditions. The authors concluded that the child's guilt in relation to the suicide was enormous and that the communication between the child and the surviving adult was distorted. They felt these factors contributed significantly to the child's problems.

Anthony (1973) writes that

> depending on their stage of development, children react to a parent's suicide with varying degrees of disbelief, of acceptance, and of ambivalence. From the child's point of view, suicide is an act of desertion that, like adoption, can never be satisfactorily accounted for, only rationalized . In some ways they are better off with a particular parent dead than alive and yet, his deadness itself may constitute a threat in making previously impossible wishes possible. . . . Suicide intensifies, and is often meant to intensify, the guilt and self-reproach of those who survive. Suicide is an act that continues its aggressive impact over long periods of time on the lives of those who survive.

In another paper, Cain and Fast (1972) contend that each child, in addition to having to cope with a loss of a parent from a suicide, must cope with

> the psychological stresses and burdens typical of parent loss: their surviving parent's shock, grief, preoccupied withdrawal, guilt and blaming; their own heightened separation problems and deep sense of loss, misconceptions and fears of death; irrational guilts; anger over desertion; distorted intertwining of the bereavement reactions of the child and surviving parent; realignments of family dynamics necessitated by the loss; stressful changes made in basic living arrangements; revival or heightening of intrapsychic conflicts and the related problems of a one-parent family.

Lindemann et al. (1972) described their preventive intervention in a four year-old boy whose father committed suicide when the child was fifteen months old. The child was identified during a routine mental health appraisal of an incoming school population. The child showed peculiar psychomotor manifestations and evidence of more apprehension and preoccupation than was the norm for his group. Play therapy was used to reduce his anxiety and to give him a better understanding of the problems of death, of loss, and of the meaning of good and bad. The authors felt that the treatment may perhaps have helped to forestall the development of his personality into the pattern of an obsessive compulsive neurosis.

Ilan (1973) describes the short term therapy of a sixteen year-old boy whose father committed suicide when the boy was ten. The boy showed no morbid reactions to the traumatic loss at the time. However, at the age of fifteen there was a pathological upsurge of feeling connected with the father's death and this was worked through in treatment. The child had not been given the opportunity to work through the experience when it happened. Ilan states that it is an open question whether better psychological management of the situation at the time could have prevented the adolescent upheaval and spared him the necessity for treatment. He suggests that preventive measures in the case of a latency loss can have only limited possibilities as long as inner feelings are covered up by a strong relationship with the remaining parent. During the developmental phase of adolescence, however, when the problems of separation and identification are again accentuated, even a relatively brief period of psychotherapy may be effective in redirecting the child along a healthier channel.

Ever since the early papers by Zilboorg (1937) which related loss of a loved object to depression and suicide, there has been considerable interest in the relationship between parental loss in childhood and later suicidal behavior.

In several studies, overt self-destructive behavior has been noted in the surviving group. Dorpat (1972) reported that out of 17 children surviving their parent's suicide, there were 5 suicide attempts and 2 suicidal deaths subsequent to the loss. In addition, subsequent depressive episodes were seen in 9 of the 17 survivors. Cain and Fast (1966) reported 4 suicide attempts and 3 suicidal deaths among 45 survivors.

Hill (1969) studied the relationship between death of a parent in childhood and a subsequent attempted suicide in adult life. His study consisted of a group of 1,483 patients who were all hospitalized for depression. He concluded that suicide is significantly more common in depressed women who lost their fathers when aged ten to fourteen, and to a lesser extent, at fifteen to nineteen. Men and women whose mothers died in the first 10 years of life also tended to attempt suicide more often.

Ilan (1973) writes that

current clinical practice in the case of families who have suffered the loss of a parent is to make sure that the children receive the necessary factual information, that they are given ample opportunity to talk about the loss, and that the feelings of the family members are not concealed from them. The rationale for the advice is based upon the alleged need of children to undergo a period of mourning with the hope that in so doing they will be spared the later development of psychopathology. More recently, however, doubts have arisen as to whether children, in fact, are able to mourn like the adult whose grief normally terminates in a nonpathological resolution of the relationship.

Dorpat (1972) reported on 17 adult patients all of whom lost a parent to suicide as children. Three were diagnosed as neurotic, nine had character disorders and five were psychotic. Pathological findings included:

1.   Guilt over the parental suicide.
2.   Depression.
3.   Morbid preoccupation with suicide.
4.   Self-destructive behavior: 5 attempts, 2 successful suicides.
5.   Absence of grief.
6.   Arrest of specific aspects of ego, superego, and libidinal development.

Intervention

Despite the lack of clear guidelines from the literature, there is sufficient knowledge at this point to outline a method to enable us to think about the problems of intervening in a child survivor of a parental suicide in a logical and well thought out way.

Because of the dramatic impact a parental suicide can

have on the family, *all* surviving children should be evaluated, counseled if age-appropriate, and given the opportunity for long-term professional follow-up care in order to help them deal immediately with the tragic event, to help place the suicide in a realistic light in which they can appropriately relate to, and to prevent, or at least minimize, the damage the suicide can have on their future development and adjustment.

I. Special Considerations for Assessment of a Child Survivor

It is difficult, if not impossible, to give a specific prescription for the intervention in, and the treatment of, a child who survives a parental suicide because there are so many variables in each case. Each variable must be carefully evaluated in order to determine how each one affects the surviving child.

1. Age of Child: Children are able to question, understand, and experience events only in relation to their level of development. Since a child's level of development is closely related to the child's chronological age, probably the single most important factor is the age of the child at the time of the parent's suicide.

A. Attachment: The age of the child will determine whether an attachment has taken place between the child and the parent. Children under the age of six months do not form attachments and any parent loss up until this age will not immediately affect the child in an untoward way. The works of Bowlby (1960) and Spitz (1965) stress the importance and strength of the child-parental bond after the age of six months.

B. Oedipal Phase: A loss of the parent of the same sex during the oedipal phase of development could, from a theoretical point of view, have disastrous consequences for the child. The child's unconscious wish to have harm done to the parent not only becomes a reality, but is accomplished in such a powerful and dramatic way by the hand of the parent, that a devastating effect on the child could be predicted.

C. Adolescent Years: During the early adolescent years of development when children are coping with the problems of dependency vs. independency, there is thought to be a re-emergence of the oedipal conflict, and a parental loss due to suicide at this stage of development will throw the normal adolescent turmoil into further conflicts and uncertainty.

D. Concept of Death: There has been some lack of clarity as to when a child comprehends the meaning of death and can view it as a permanent and irreversible loss of a loved one. Piaget (1960) felt that children begin to develop a realistic concept of death around the age of six and that the development is completed by the age of eleven or twelve when the finality of death is recognized.

Some investigators maintain that a child is not able properly to mourn for a parent until adolescence (Nagera, 1970) when there is a more realistic concept of death, when there is the re-emergence of the oedipal conflict and the problems of independence vs. dependence arise.

E. Concept of Suicide: Equally important is the child's view of the meaning of suicidal behavior (Orbach & Glaubman, 1968). This is a more difficult problem to study. As researchers, we are as yet unclear what a parental suicide specifically means to a child at various stages of development, but we can construct some generalizations based upon our understanding of normal development. A child receives ego support, structure, love, and role-modeling among other features from a parent and the removal of these necessary supports by a suicide leaves the child bewildered, confused, vulnerable, uncertain, and unsure of his/her own impulse control and magical thoughts.

2. When and How Child Finds out about the Parental Suicide

The way in which the child first finds out about the parental suicide is another significant variable that must be taken into consideration as part of the total evaluation. Some children are told that their parent committed suicide several years after the event. These children can be informed about it from surviving relatives or discover the facts themselves by overhearing family conversations or reading papers or documents found in the house. Others are told immediately following the event. Others can hear the parent in the act of suicide, while others may actually witness it. Other children may discover the body and still others, the most unfortunate, may actually help in the suicide act. There is, on occasion, the extra burden of the survivor of a murder-suicide in which one parent kills his or her spouse and perhaps one or more children before killing himself or herself. A child witnessing or surviving this type of incident could predictably develop different kinds of problems than a child who is told of a parental suicide several hours or days after the event.

In one study, Andress and Corey (1978) examined 1,092 suicides committed in Riverside County, California between 1960–1974 to establish who witnessed suicides. Of the 1,092 cases, 259 were classified as witnessed suicides and of the 259, 72 children witnessed their parent's suicide.

Children should be told that their parent died and that the death was the result of a suicidal act as soon after the incident as possible. Close family members, who themselves are grieving appropriately, and who feel comfortable doing so, should explain to children in terms that they can understand the circumstances of the death. It is usually tragic and terribly unfair for a child to discover the true facts from people outside of the family unit.

II. Assessment

Before a therapeutic intervention can be implemented, a detailed and thorough assessment of the problem must be undertaken. The purpose of this assessment is to evaluate the dimensions of the problem, to determine what strengths and weaknesses are present in the child and in the family, and to attempt to formulate a working understanding of the emotional dynamics within the child and family.

1. *Family*: As part of the assessment procedure all surviving family members should be screened and evaluated to determine not only the status of their mental health and their own need for intervention, but to determine which of these members could be relied upon as a resource to help the child over the mourning period. Family dynamics are most important to formulate in order to understand the role that the child plays in the house. It is necessary to understand how each member feels about the victim and how each views the suicide within the family constellation.

2. *Child's Personality prior to the Suicide*: An indication as to how a child will handle the grief process may be gained by an assessment of his/her personality prior to the suicide. A child who has had a normal emotional development and who had been relatively free of any emotional problems will probably have a better chance of handling a parental loss than a child who had exhibited signs of emotional problems prior to the loss.

3. *Pre-Suicide Personality of the Victim-Parent*: Frequently the parent who commits suicide has had a history of overt psychological problems.

According to a World Health Organization (1968) report, the estimate of the frequency of mental disorders in completed suicides ranges from 20 to 94 percent. However, each country reporting in the study had its own definition of mental illness. Some limited it to psychosis, while others included neurosis and personality disorders. Still others relied on their own clinical impressions as to what constituted mental illness.

On the basis of clinical history, Dorpat and Ripley (1960) in one study of completed suicides and Barraclough et al. (1968) in another study judged 90 percent of the victims to have been mentally ill. In a report of 11 studies of attempted suicide, Stengel (1950) estimated the incidence of mental illness to be 100 percent.

An evaluation of the parent's personality is clearly necessary in order to help understand the pattern of relationships within the family prior to the event. Frequently, the children are intimately involved in the parent's illness, and understanding the dynamics is a vital part of the intervention process. For example, the parent may have been moody, depressed, and withdrawn; or belligerent, argumentative, critical, and assaultive; or the parent could have been grossly psychotic, irrational, causing much turmoil within the family.

This information is useful not only in shedding light on the family dynamics but is needed in evaluating how the child viewed the parent who suicided and the nature of the emotional attachment which was present prior to the suicide. The deliberateness of purpose in suicidal death intensifies the feelings of the involvement in the survivors.

4. *Behavior and Mood of the Child*: Whenever the child is first seen, whether it be hours or even years after the suicide, an evaluation of the child's behavior, mood, thinking, and functioning is necessary before a meaningful intervention can be undertaken.

Children's symptoms will depend on:

(a)   the child's age.
(b)   pre-suicide personality of child.

Children's symptoms can be divided into the following (which necessarily overlap):

(a) Neurotic: anxiety, depression, somatic complaints, phobias, obsessive-compulsive traits.
(b) Psychotic: delusions, hallucinations. A psychotic child may wish to join dead parent; or may hear the dead parent calling; or may see the dead parent in a vision.
(c) Behavioral: hyperactivity, hypoactivity; sleeping, eating, bowel, or bladder disturbance; tics, or unusual habits or mannerisms.
(d) School-related problems: poor attendance, poor grades, lack of interest, daydreaming, behavioral problems.

An assessment *must* be made of the following:

(a) Child's understanding of death and dying in general, and of suicide in particular.
(b) Child's current functioning.
(c) Child's weaknesses and strengths.
(d) Child's tendency to self-destructive behavior.
(e) Child's preoccupation with suicide.
(f) Absence or presence of a grief process.

III. Treatment

A. *Treatment Plan*: After a careful assessment, a treatment plan should be outlined with the goals of:

1. Helping the child over the acute stage of grief.

2. Helping child work through feelings toward dead parent.
3. Helping the child to reach an understanding of the suicidal death that preserves the sense of self-worth and satisfies the search for meaning.
4. Helping the child realistically plan for a future without the dead parent.

B. *Treatment Method*:

1. All children should be seen and followed up. They should be allowed to ventilate whatever they wish in a supportive and receptive atmosphere. Their interpretation of and their role in the events leading up to the suicide give important information as to how they may view the tragedy.
2. The therapist should help the child deal with the normal grief process of anger, depression, bewilderment. In other words, the child should be encouraged to mourn the loss in a healthy manner.
3. The therapist must always keep in mind that he/she cannot be a substitute for the lost parent.
4. Always assume that guilt is present. An idea frequently expressed by the surviving child is that he or she caused the suicide by being bad, or could have saved the parent either by being good or by some heroic act. This guilt can be reinforced directly or subtly by other surviving family members.
5. Throughout the therapy one should be alert for the development of the symptoms as

outlined previously in the areas of mood, behavior, functioning, or thought.

6. Assume that a heightened fear of abandonment is present. The fear of abandonment is one of the most frightening fears of childhood and a loss of a parent early in life, especially from a suicidal act, only serves to reinforce this fear and the child's normal insecurities.

7. In many children, the fear of losing control and committing suicide is present. The therapist must deal with the child's own fear of following in the parent's footsteps; the fear of also losing control someday and perhaps taking his or her own life.

8. The question of the inheritance of suicidal traits is frequently posed by the surviving child, and the therapist must help the child deal with this issue.

9. Encourage honest communication within the family. There is a tendency in many families to cover up information, to lie to the child, to give the child wrong or partial information with the good intentions of protecting the child (Pruett, 1978). It is extremely difficult to explain away a lie to a child. A lie only causes more suspicion, more anxiety, and in itself represents an additional problem which the child will have to overcome at a time when he or she needs full emotional resources to cope with the loss.

10. Use family members to help child cope. Family members who seem to have a good grasp of the situation and who can handle

their own mourning process appropriately should be encouraged to spend time or speak with the surviving child.

11. Careful periodic follow-up. The child should be encouraged to call the therapist should the need arise. Questions may develop as the child matures and the child should feel there is a resource on whom he or she can rely should difficulties arise after the initial treatment period.

Sibling Suicide:

Another dimension to the problem, which will be mentioned briefly, not because it is unimportant but because so little attention has been focused on it, is the child survivor of a sibling suicide (Rudestam, 1975). With the teenage-suicide rate on the rise, the number of child survivors of this type of suicide has also risen. But here again, the literature is painfully lacking even in anecdotal reports. The pain and suffering is overwhelming, but we as professionals do not have as yet the body of knowledge available to permit us to intervene in an intelligent way. However, that is not to say we should not intervene, because we do have general concepts which permit us to help all children in crisis situations.

Conclusions:

At the present time, and until well-designed studies are performed, we will not know which psychological interventions are efficacious in preventing psychiatric difficulties later on in life in this population of children. It is clear that more research is needed in the following areas:

1. We need to have a better understanding of the child's reaction to suicide at each level of development.

2. We need to have better ideas to help us intervene in the acute phase of the grieving process.

3. We need to have psychological markers to enable us to identify and treat the vulnerable child.

4. We need to know which symptoms should alert us to the possibility of the development of problems later on in life.

5. We need a method to help identify these children who will repeat the parental act as adults.

6. We need to study those children who successfully adjust to a parental suicide and attempt to use the mechanism of their success to help other children to cope better.

7. We need to know whether special intervention techniques are needed with respect to the sex of the child and the parent.

8. Lastly, we should insist that suicide statistics list whether the victim had children and should indicate the age and sex of the children in order for these statistics to have any meaning for investigators studying the impact of a suicide in a family on the surviving children.

We can safely say that the impact of a parental suicide on the surviving children can be catastrophic, and that the emotional scars last well into adulthood. We must intervene in all cases and use our current knowledge to help ease the initial shock of the tragedy and to help normalize future growth and development. However, we should strive to obtain specific knowledge with respect to these types of suicides so that we can intervene with proven ideas and proven methods.

REFERENCES

Andress, V.R., & Corey, D.M. Survivor-victims of suicides: Who discovers or witnesses suicide? *Psychological Reports*, 1978, *42*, 759-764.

Anthony, E.J. Editorial Comment. In E.J. Anthony & C. Koupernik (Eds.), *The child & his family* (Vol. II). New York: Wiley, 1973.

Barraclough, B.M., Nelson, B., & Sainbury, P. The diagnostic classification and psychiatric treatment of 25 suicides. In N.L. Farberow (Ed.), *Proceedings of the Fourth International Conference for Suicide Prevention Center*, Los Angeles: Delmar Publishing Co., 1968.

Bendiksen, R., & Fulton, R. Death and the child: An anterospective test of the childhood bereavement and later behavior disorder hypothesis. *Omega*, 1965, *6*(I), 45-59.

Bowlby, J. Grief and mourning in infancy and early childhood. *The Psychoanalytic Study of the Child*, 1960, *15*, 9-52.

Bowlby, J. Childhood mourning and its implications for psychiatry. *American Journal of Psychiatry*, 1961, *118*, 481-498.

Brown, G., Harris, T., & Copeland, R. Depression and loss. *British Journal of Psychiatry*, 1977, *130*, 1-18.

Cain, A., & Fast, I. Children's disturbed reactions to parent suicide: Distortions of quiet, communications and identification. In A. Cain (Ed.) *Survivors of Suicidal Death*. Springfield: Charles Thomas, 1972.

Deutsch, H. Absence of grief. *Psychoanalytic Quarterly*, 1937, *9*, 12-22.

Dorpat, T.L. Psychological effects of parental suicide on surviving children. In A. Cain (Ed.), *Survivors of Suicidal Death*. Springfield: Charles Thomas, 1972.

Dorpat, T.L. & Ripley, H.S. A study of suicide in the Seattle area. *Comprehensive Psychiatry*, 1960, *1*, 349-359.

Freud, S. Mourning & melancholia. *Collected Papers* (Vol. 4). New York: Basic Books, 1959.

Hill, O.W. The association of childhood bereavement with suicidal attempt in depressive illness. *British Journal of Psychiatry*, 1969, *520*, 301-304.

Ilan, E. The impact of a father's suicide on his latency son. In E. Anthony & C. Koupernik (Eds.) *The Child and His Family (Vol. II)*. New York: Wiley, 1973.

Klein, M. A contribution to the theory of anxiety and guilt. *International Journal of Psychiatry*, 1978, *29*, 114-123.

Kliman, G. *Psychological emergencies of childhood*, New York: Grune & Stratton, 1968.

Kübler-Ross, E. *On death and dying*, New York: Macmillan, 1969.

Lindemann, E., Vaughan, W., & McGinnes, M. Preventive intervention in a four year old child whose father committed suicide. In A. Cain (Ed.), *Survivors of Suicidal Death*. Springfield: Charles Thomas, 1972.

Linzer, N. (Ed.). *Understanding bereavement and grief*, New York: KTAV, 1977.

Lopez, T., & Kliman, G.W. Memory, recognition, and mourning in the analysis of a four year old child. *The Psychoanalytic Study of the Child*, 1979, *34*, 235-271.

Markusen, E., & Fulton, R. Childhood bereavement and behavior disorders: A critical review. *Omega*, 1971, *2*, 107-117.

Nagera, H. Children's reactions to the death of important objects, *The Psychoanalytic Study of the Child*, 1970, *25*, 360-400.

Orbach, I., & Glaubman, H. The concept of death and suicidal behavior in young children, *Journal of the American Academy of Child Psychiatry*, 1968, *18*, 668-678.

Pfeffer, C.R., Conte, H.R., Plutchik, R., & Jerrett, M.A. Suicidal behavior in latency age children. *Journal of the American Academy of Child Psychiatry*, 1980, *19*(4), 703-710.

Piaget, J. *The child's conception of the world*, Totowa, N.J.: Adams, 1960.

Pruett, K.D. Home treatment for two infants who witnessed their mother's murder. *Journal of the American Academy of Child Psychiatry*, 1979, *18*(4), 647-657.

Roy, A. Role of past loss in depression. *Archives of General Psychiatry*, 1981, *38*, 301-302.

Rudestam, K.E. Effects of suicide on survivors. In *Proceedings of the Eighth Annual Meeting, American Association of Suicidology*, B. Comstock & R. Maris (Eds.). St. Louis, Mo: 1975.

Spitz, R. *The first year of life.* New York: International Universities Press, 1965.

Stengel, E. Classification of mental disorders. *Bulletin of the World Health Organization*, 1960, *21*, 601-663.

Volkart, E.H., & Michael, S.T. Bereavement and mental health. In A.H. Leighton, J.A. Clausen, & R.N. Wilson (Eds.), *Explorations in social psychiatry.* New York: Basic Books, 1957.

Wekstein, L. *Handbook of suicidology,* New York: Brunner/Mazel, 1979.

The World Almanac & Book of Facts, 1979, Newspaper Enterprise Association, New York, 1978.

World Health Statistics Annuals, Geneva: World Health Organization, *21* (6), 1968.

Zilboorg, G. Considerations on suicide with particular reference to that of the young. *American Journal of Orthopsychiatry*, 1937, 9.

Chapter 12

CRISIS: PSYCHOLOGICAL FIRST AID FOR RECOVERY AND GROWTH

Ann S. Kliman

Suicide is death by design. That is the only statement I can make about it without qualification, for the complexities of suicidal motivations and reactions are so profound as to leave all generalities open to argument. Except for military and rescue operations in which electing to die is deemed heroic, suicide has been viewed in our society as shameful, so shameful that families, clergy, police, and physicians often attempt to keep the manner of such deaths hidden and speak rather of "accidents."

Increasing attention has been paid to the phenomenon of suicide over the past several years. Dozens of studies conducted by physicians, therapists, sociologists, and federal agencies have made us aware of suicide as a major public health issue. We have learned that a large proportion of automobile accidents are disguised suicides. We have learned, but find it most difficult to believe, that children between three and twelve deliberately consider and do commit suicide. And we have learned that suicide, like child abuse and alcoholism, tends to be passed down to the next generation, not via the genes but by unconscious identification with the willfully abandoning parent.

The method of suicide can tell us a great deal about the dead person's motives. Violent and self-mutilating suicides (jumping from heights, shooting through the head, slashing wrists, and so forth) clearly demonstrate both rage turned inward toward the self and rage turned outward toward survivors. The discovery of such disfigured, bloody bodies is horrifying. Self-hanging usually reflects the victim's wish to be punished—and to punish. Self-immolation is a violent statement of rage, helplessness, and a demand to excite guilt in others. Drug overdoses, or combinations of pills and alchohol, are perhaps the "gentlest" method of suicide, but may be made violent by accusatory notes left to family, colleagues, or friends. One-vehicle "accidents" often combine ambivalent feelings of anger (in the mutilation of the body) and protectiveness (it will seem an accident; insurance will be paid) toward the family. A suicide involving two or more vehicles expresses literal murderous rage.

Whether or not any person has the "right" to commit suicide is a question that has been debated over the centuries by theologians, legislators, therapists, sociologists, and philosophers. I have no answer for anyone but myself. I can imagine that in circumstances such as loss of brain function, chronic and unrelievable severe pain, or total isolation, I would wish to die and would design my own death. Such real situations would be intolerable for me, and I believe I would have the right to make a decision to end them for myself. I would never try to impose that belief on anyone else.

All of us who have worked with people who express

suicidal ideas have learned to take them seriously, and to assess carefully the profundity and intensity of the idea. Suicidal ideas may be manipulative, neurotic, psychotic, reactive, or realistic. Such despairing comments as "I can't go on" or "I wish I were dead" indicate a person at risk who is pleading for help. These people cannot be helped by "That's ridiculous!" "Don't talk like that!" "Look at all you have to live for," or, most damaging of all, by ignoring their plea. Potential suicides at highest risk are those who not only say they wish to die, but also have a plan worked out. Often we can assist such people to find other less drastic and irrevocable alternatives; sometimes we cannot.

It is true that people who are determined to die will find a way despite the most intensive care, tight restraints, and careful observation. Except for disaster survivors and the bereaved—people in a reactive depression appropriate and expectable following an acute loss (and as such frequently accessible to brief intervention that facilitates mourning)—I have had little experience with people who threaten or attempt suicide. I have had considerable experience working with the families of people who have committed suicide. Without exception, the surviving spouse, children, and parents react with pervasive guilt, conscious and unconscious, which makes them particularly vulnerable to expiatory acts of self-punishment including accidents, illnesses, and breakdowns in family relationships.

Of all deaths, the most difficult to understand, and the most psychologically agonizing, is the suicide of a child. The death of a child from any cause makes a parent feel helpless. Functioning is impaired as one's sense of reliability and dependability plummet, and a child's suicide makes parents feel malignantly irresponsible and culpable. There is no disease, no reckless driver, piece of machinery, or natural disaster to blame. One's guilt precludes blaming the child, who is seen as "too young." The parents must blame themselves. I say "must," for the implacability of such parental guilt is awesome.

Jason Reynolds was fourteen when he took his father's gun and shot himself in the head. His suicide note read simply,"Dear Mom and Dad, I'm a born loser. I can't take it anymore. I'm sorry. You'll be better off without me. Love, Jason." The shot awoke nine year-old Gerry in the next room. He ran into his brother's room to find him lying bloody and mutilated on the bed. Gerry's screams brought Howard and Joanne Reynolds racing in from the living room where they had been watching TV. Pushing Gerry and his mother out of the room and locking the door, Mr. Reynolds tried desperately to revive Jason. But he knew it was hopeless. The .38 caliber gun had blown off the back of Jason's head. Dimly, through his shocked, disbelieving horror, Mr. Reynolds became aware of his younger son's shouting to his mother to wake up, and to his father for help. He covered Jason and went in the direction of the shouting to find his wife unconscious on the floor of their bedroom, with Gerry trying vainly to lift her into a sitting position. Without a word, Howard Reynolds lifted his wife onto the bed, brought a wet washcloth and put it on her forehead, then took Gerry by the hand and started for the front door. Gerry was crying and protesting and trying to pull away from his father. He kept crying that Jason and his mother were both dead. Mr. Reynolds held tightly to Gerry's hand and reassured him that his mother had just fainted and would be all right. He also told Gerry he was taking him to stay with the Fells, their next-door neighbors and good friends. Mr. Fell welcomed Gerry without any comment except that Gerry was always welcome. Mr. Reynolds left them. Within less than 15 minutes Gerry had been abandoned by his brother, his mother, and finally his father.

I didn't see Gerry until the day after the funeral, and I saw him then only because he precipitated the referral.

Gerry had been kept at the neighbors throughout the 3 days between his brother's suicide and the funeral. His father visited him daily, but refused to allow him to return home because "everything is so chaotic" and "the Fells are taking very good care of you." The night his brother died, Gerry watched a stream of people entering and leaving his home. He saw Jason's body carried out on a stretcher, he saw the doctor arrive and the light go on in his parents' bedroom; he saw two policemen, the minister, his grandparents, his uncles, and some people he couldn't identify; but he did not see his mother. When his father visited him the following morning, Gerry begged to see his mother, but Mr. Reynolds refused, saying that his mother was too sedated but that he could see her in a few days. Gerry asked about Jason, but his father only kept repeating, "The gun must have gone off while he was cleaning it." Gerry didn't believe him. He knew Jason, and Jason hated guns. He'd never spend a second cleaning a gun. Gerry also knew his father. Mr. Reynolds had taught his sons to respect guns, always to check to make sure a gun wasn't loaded before cleaning or even handling it. The gun case was always locked and there was only one key, kept under his father's socks in his bureau. Jason would have had to have stolen the key to get the gun. Most importantly, Gerry had seen the note. If his father had lied about Jason, maybe he was lying about his mother, too. Gerry made several attempts to sneak back into his own home, but each time he was found by someone and returned to the neighbors—before he could see his mother. On the day of the funeral Gerry dutifully left the Fells' house for school, carrying his lunch bag and books. A block away he hid them in the bushes and found a phone booth. He called the funeral home he had heard Mrs. Fell mention on the phone and found out the time of the service. For the first time since his brother's suicide, Gerry was given the information he was seeking.

It was a very long walk. Gerry wanted to take his bike, but there was no way to get it out of the garage without being seen. He didn't dare hitch a ride; someone might ask him why he wasn't in school. He arrived at the funeral home at 10:30, a half hour before the service. He didn't know what he was going to do—he just knew he had to see Jason once more, and he had to see his mother.

At that moment a group of teenagers came in. Gerry melted into the group and walked with them to see Jason. But the casket was closed. What if there'd been a mistake, what if it weren't Jason in there? Gerry stroked the smooth wood and tried to remember how Jason had looked. He wondered if Jason was still all bloody. He was very frightened. Then a man came in and asked everyone to leave, announcing that the family wanted to be alone for a while. Gerry tried to hide himself among the kids, but suddenly he saw his parents as they saw him. His mother was walking in tiny steps, collapsed against his father. Her face was hidden behind a heavy veil. She screamed! And began to sob. His father's face tightened. "What are you doing here! You are supposed to be in school."

"Don't be mad, Dad, please. I had to say goodbye to Jase, Dad, I had to. Please, please don't be mad." His mother reached out her arms and Gerry ran to her. Hugging and rocking, they sobbed together. It was the first time Gerry had been able to cry. Mr. Reynolds enfolded his wife and son in his arms, his face turned away so they could not see his tears.

Gerry didn't understand the funeral. Someone talked about "infinite wisdom," "mysterious ways," "the grief-stricken parents," "the bereft younger brother." No one talked about Jason. Now, with both parents crying, Gerry couldn't cry. He wondered what was the matter with him. He reached for his mother's hand, but she was holding herself as if she thought she would fall apart if she let go. He turned to his father, but before he could say a word he was told to be quiet and not upset his mother anymore. Gerry kept quiet.

Gerry remained quiet until his father brought him to see me the following day. On the phone Mr. Reynolds told me he was so worried about the way Gerry had "acted up," that he was following his minister's advice to "get help for Gerry." I told him I would like to see Gerry with both his parents. Mr. Reynolds refused. "My wife is much too upset, too heavily sedated. She doesn't have the strength to see you." I volunteered to come to the house. "This is a time when you all need one another very much. It is very important for your family to stay together. My job is not to further upset Mrs. Reynolds, it is to help her cope with what is already upsetting her so desperately." Howard Reynolds was adamant; he would come with Gerry, but he would not bring his wife. I accepted his terms, hoping I would have a chance when we met to help him understand that his seemingly protective attitude was only making his wife less able to cope with Jason's suicide.

Within seconds of meeting me, Gerry began to talk. He told me everything I've reported to this point; the words poured out of him without a stop, even when his father interjected a statement of explanation. He told me how terrified he had been, how he was sure until he saw her that his mother was dead too. He said he couldn't get "the sight of all the blood out of my head."

I nodded. "You can't get the sight of all the blood out of your head just like you couldn't make all the blood on Jason's head disappear. You have all kinds of frightening thoughts and questions about death. You can't make yourself stop thinking about him. This is a good place to talk about all the ideas that are worrying and frightening you."

He turned to his father. "Dad, don't get mad, please. I know Jason wasn't cleaning the gun. I saw the note. Why did you lie to me? Why did he do it? Why, Dad? Tell me!"

Mr. Reynolds whispered, "I didn't believe it. I thought you wouldn't know. I'm sorry, Gerry, maybe I shouldn't have lied to you. But I'm not lying now. I don't know why he did it. God help me! I'm his father and I don't know why my son killed himself. Why couldn't he have come to me? Why didn't I know how desperate he was? God forgive me, Joanne never will. And I'll never forgive myself!"

I didn't know whom to attend to first. I decided to attend to them together. "It seems you're both expressing the same feelings in different ways. Gerry, twice in the last 20 minutes you've seemed afraid your dad would get mad at you. I wonder, does your dad get mad at you often—is that really what's making you afraid?"

They both looked at me in surprise and shook their heads.

"No," Gerry said, "Dad almost never gets mad at me. Sometimes he gets annoyed, but not really mad like Jase did."

"That's a very important thing to know. You have lots of thoughts of someone getting mad, but you know your dad rarely gets mad. Then you remember Jason got mad a lot. Maybe you got mad at him too. Maybe you feel as any brother would—you have an angry feeling toward Jason for killing himself, for doing it in such a horrifying way, even for deserting you. For most of us it's too frightening to think angrily about the dead, it's too scary to remember their anger; but all those angry thoughts have to go somewhere, and it's safe to think about your dad being angry because you're not really scared of him. Mr. Reynolds, you too have very angry feelings. But you turn your anger back on yourself. You blame yourself for 'not

knowing,' for not having been able to prevent Jason's suicide. You are angrily punishing yourself as if you had the
power to have known and stopped Jason. You say your
wife won't ever forgive you either. That may or may not
be true, but as long as she is isolated at home and so sedated
that she cannot think clearly or share her grief, it will continue to remain inside her. The tranquilizers and sleeping
pills cannot remove her pain; they can only delay it. As
angry as you are with yourself, so she must be angry at
herself; only you express it openly, she expresses it by with-
drawing."

Mr. Reynolds nodded slowly. "You can't know what
it's been like. She's been a zombie. I know she blames me,
she'd have to. It was my gun, and she hated guns. But I
never used them carelessly. And I only hunted for food,
never just to kill. But my gun killed Jason. I was his father.
It was my responsibility to protect him, not to set him up
to commit suicide. Why didn't I know?"

"Mr. Reynolds, I know nothing about Jason except
what I have learned just now, that he was angry very often.
For us even to begin to understand why he decided to kill
himself, we are going to have to take a hard look at him.
I will need to hear about him from all of you. We may or
may not be able to understand his decision, you all may or
may not have had a role in his decision, but I am sure of
one thing—that you are all acting self-destructively, almost
as if you were trying to get closer to Jason by being as self-
hurtful as he was. I wonder if that's the only or the best
way to mourn Jason. I think not. But to find other ways
we must work together. You will need to remember all of
Jason, not just his self-destruction. Mr. Reynolds, I would
like to see you, your wife, and Gerry tomorrow. We have
a great deal of hard work to do, and the sooner we begin
the greater chance we have to do it well."

As they left the room Gerry turned back toward me

and said, "I am mad at Jason. He shouldn't have done this, not to us, not to him. He shouldn't have done it!"

"Gerry, Jason must have been hurting very much to have hurt you and your parents so badly. But you have every right to be angry at him. That's something we can talk more about tomorrow. I'll see you then."

I saw the Reynoldses the next day, then twice a week for slightly more than a year, and came to learn a great deal about Jason, the family history, and the family "secrets." Jason was described by his parents and brother as a "wonderful kid . . . until a year ago." Mrs. Reynolds said he was a warm, friendly, mischievous boy who was, however, very sensitive. Mr. Reynolds agreed, adding "and he was wonderful with his hands, he could build anything, fix anything, and he was a really good tennis player." Gerry described his brother as having been "awfully bossy," but always ready to help him build models, help him with his homework, and even let him tag along with his friends. All agreed Jason was a perfectionist. Until a year ago. Then Jason changed. He became moody, was often withdrawn, flew off the handle "at nothing," and his grades dropped from honors to barely passing. His parents recalled that a lot was happening at the time. Jason was entering puberty, his body was changing rapidly, and he often complaned his knees hurt, his legs ached, he "looked weird," and he "hated" how skinny and gangly he was. He began complaining that he was a "weirdo" and that no one understood him. About the same time his maternal grandfather had a coronary attack and died. Jason had been quite close to his grandfather and seemed devastated by the loss. Several weeks later a close friend of Jason's was killed in a bike accident, then a tennis acquaintance had a leg amputated because of a lymphosarcoma.

Jason's withdrawal deepened. He avoided family meals and get-togethers; when he did join in he was provocative, irritable, and preoccupied with bodily complaints and the "uselessness of life." He would "spoil the fun" the family used to have with his "morbid preoccupation" with accidents, illness, skyjackings, kidnappings, pollution, street crime, and the "stupidity of the world." His parents tried to be patient, tried to talk with him, but he pushed them away. They thought it was just a "stage;" after all, "all adolescents have a rough time." From morbid concern about the stupidity of the world, Jason moved to constant criticism of his own inadequacies. He couldn't concentrate in school, he was "dumb." His coordination was "off," he played "lousy tennis." He was always tired, nothing interested him anymore. Increasingly concerned, his parents took him to his pediatrician who reported that Jason was slightly underweight, probably from poor eating habits like most teenagers, but was essentially healthy. "No cause for concern." They were also told that he was in an early but rapid growth spurt, and that he'd be fine when he hit his stride.

Both parents expressed how helpless they felt during this time. Jason seemed unreachable. "Just leave me alone! . . . Don't bother about me!" became the sum of his communication. Gerry was often the butt of his anger. He constantly criticized Gerry for being lazy and irresponsible, a "pig;" and Gerry retaliated by calling Jason a "dumb weirdo." Again Mr. and Mrs. Reynolds sought help. They spoke to the guidance counselor at school, who agreed with their concern about Jason's school work but suggested that they were overanxious. The pediatrician also said he'd be glad to talk to Jason, but Jason refused to see him. They then consulted with a psychiatrist, who felt Jason's withdrawal and preoccupations with his "inadequacies" indicated a problem of greater severity than the expectable difficulties of adolescence, and recommended an evaluation for Jason. After much argument, Jason agreed to go, but managed to "forget" the appointment. Two days later he killed himself. No one at home, school, or among his friends knew of "anything special" that had occurred during those 2 days. No major crises, losses, or disappointments were discovered to give a clue to the timing of Jason's decision to kill himself. Long accustomed to his "morbid preoccupations," no one had noticed anything different in his communications or his behavior. His suicide was a shock to everyone.

Over the next few weeks, Mr. and Mrs. Reynolds were enmeshed in self-recriminations and angry accusations. They tried not to argue in front of Gerry, but a closed bedroom door was poor insulation for their pain and rage. Night after night Gerry overheard their shouts and sobs. They tried to be helpful by assuring him he was not responsible for his brother's problems or actions, but by then both had lost faith in their ability to parent, to protect, and to nurture their son. Their assurances sounded hollow to Gerry, who felt his world crumbling around him.

That the family continued to come regularly to their scheduled appointments was the only sign I saw for hope of their eventual return to healthy functioning. My work during this time revolved primarily around confronting them with how, in their grief and guilt, they were alienating themselves from one another in much the same way Jason had alienated himself from them. I acknowledged how hard they had tried to get help for Jason and pointed out that he had refused it. Now they were seeking help for themselves, but they were not allowing themselves or each other the closeness and sharing that would facilitate their healing. Each of their painful, angry actions and reactions was a reliving, an imitation, of the last year of Jason's life. It was as if they were saying, "Since I couldn't make Jason's life happy, I will never allow myself to be happy either."

It was several months before Mrs. Reynolds allowed herself to enter Jason's bedroom. She found a notebook and bottles of amphetamines and barbiturates secreted among his records and tapes. The pills were a shock. No one had suspected Jason of being "on uppers and downers," medication that if taken indiscriminately only serves to upset the body's biochemistry and increase both irritability and depression. But it was the notebook that truly exposed him—revealing as it did the vital clue to Jason's motive.

The handwritten journal had been begun nearly a year before Jason's suicide. It was filled with wrenching descriptions of how disappointed Jason felt about his body, his character, his achievements, and his acceptability to himself, his family, and the world. Each searing self-denigration was followed by "Jimmy never would have turned out like me," or "Jimmy would've had all his shit together," or "They lost the wrong one," or "I can't ever be what Jimmy was."

Who was Jimmy? Slowly, in whispers, their voices hollow with the echo of unresolved grief, Howard and Joanne Reynolds told me about Jimmy. I could feel their anguish. Jimmy had been their first-born child. A handsome, sturdy, happy child, he filled his parents' world with joy. Then suddenly, at four and a half, Jimmy developed a high fever, and 36 hours later he was dead. The Reynoldses were incapacitated with grief. How to explain to family and friends, "there was nothing anyone could do." How could life ever be worthwhile again? Protective friends, feeling Mrs. Reynolds would be "overwhelmed," urged her husband to keep her heavily sedated and away from Jimmy's funeral. Everyone had the same advice. "You're both still young. Time will heal. Have another baby as soon as possible." Sixteen months later they did. Jason was their replacement child, but Jason was never told about Jimmy. At least no one ever sat down and spoke to him directly about Jimmy. But Jason knew and lived with the secret burden of the "ghost" of his unknown brother. We will never know how many times the secret of Jimmy's existence leaked out in overheard words, in mixed messages, in subtle pressures; we do know Jason knew. His notebook was filled with the idealized Jimmy. And the unrealized Jason.

Ultimately there was no understanding the multiplicity of events, reactions, and fantasies that eventuated in Jason's decision to commit suicide. I do not believe that any one variable was the explanation. What we know is that all the variables somehow overloaded Jason to the point where he felt so helpless and hopeless that life had lost its value. As his parents were victimized by the death of their first-born, so Jason was victimized by being unable to live up to the expectations he projected upon his parents; and by the competition with a long-dead, never-to-be-matched older sibling.

One question was left to be answered. Why did he choose the time that he did? What was its meaning? All of us who work with families in which there is a death by de-sign look for anniversary reactions. The timing of a suicide is rarely incidental. It was the awareness of the power of such anniversary reactions, rather than brilliant intuition, that led me to ask the Reynoldses for the date on which Jimmy died. It was May 1. Jason killed himself on May 1.

None of these secrets emerged until 4 months after Jason's death. They helped explain the extraordinary resis-tance the Reynoldses had shown to mourning adaptively together. Unable to do the work of mourning for Jimmy, and thus to develop some immunization to the pathogenic aspects of future losses, they succumbed to the "guilt of the survivor," and like Jason, they were overloaded. Vic-timized by Jimmy's death, they received no adequate assist-ance in coping with their loss. Indeed they were encouraged to deny and avoid, rather than cope. Jason's suicide confirmed their most terrifying nightmare: they were incompetent, inadequate, destructive parents. No wonder they had abandoned Gerry psychologically; they felt they could only harm him too. It took many more months of work to sift through all the factors involved in their double bereavement. They needed to sort out factors beyond their control: Jimmy's untreatable illness and death, the death of Jason's grandfather and friend, Jason's developmental vulnerability as an adolescent, his pill-popping. They needed to recognize that they had made misjudgments in not sharing their "terrible secret." They needed to recognize that they were not omnipotent, that all their parental power was not sufficient to make Jason want to help himself. Once these needs were acknowledged, the agonizing work of mourning could begin under healthier, more adaptive, less punitive terms. As the sole surviving child, Gerry was at high risk. He needed to define himself as Gerry, not as a magical replacement for either Jason or Jimmy. And he needed his parents' support, to accept and love him for what he was—not for what his brothers were, or were thought to be.

Gerry is now fifteen. He has outlived the ages of Jimmy and Jason. In most areas he has mastered the dangers of being a survivor because he knows he is a survivor. He has the option of returning for help when things get rough, or when he feels frightened or depressed and can't quite figure out what's troubling him. He knows it is not his weakness that he is a survivor, it is his strength and that he dares to deal with his status. Mr. and Mrs. Reynolds have done better than I would have predicted; they have learned to share their grief, guilt, and pain rather than use these feelings to punish themselves or each other. They are now able to invest their energy in helping Gerry grow increasingly strong. I don't believe they have resolved all their problems; I doubt they ever will. But they are functioning as a couple, as parents, and in their network of friends and work. And they are willing to bear the pain and enjoy the pleasure that go with being alive.

Many suicides cannot be prevented, but I am convinced it is possible to prevent the recurrence of suicide among those who survive, who feel themselves abandoned. Such prevention is not simply a matter of clinical intervention, but also of demanding better public education and social change. As long as our culture judges suicide as a sin or otherwise shameful, we will continue to impose the burdens of prolonged denial, avoidance, and maladaptive mourning practices upon the bereaved. Until our population is educated and sensitized to recognizing the vulnerabilities of those abandoned through suicide, we will continue to doom the survivors to repeat what has been inflicted on them. Again, it is not the sins of the fathers that are visited upon the children, it is the unresolved conflicts and guilts and fears of our families. We have a choice to identify with life or with death, with gratification or with loss, with productivity or stagnation, love or hate. We need courage to choose.

Chapter 13

A MOTHER'S PERSONAL EXPERIENCE IN THE LOSS OF A SON THROUGH SUICIDE

Iris M. Bolton

I have come here with a willingness to share and to be open about my life and my experiences. I have been the perfect mother and the perfect wife. I was an actress in New York City, years ago, doing gigs, soap operas, movies, and acting, and really enjoyed it. I had thought that if I were a perfect mother I would have perfect children, and if I did all the right things then everything would turn out right. I was a super mom. I was the team mother for every sport my four sons were in; I played the guitar and I sang in their classrooms from kindergarten on. I enjoyed my children.

This presentation had invited questions and answers from the audience.

We have a cabin at Lake Burton in the north Georgia woods, with no television and no telephone. We would go up on many weekends from spring through summer, the four boys, my husband, and I. We would do a lot of family things together. We are a close family and we worked at it. I've been married for 28 years. It's been a marriage that I have worked at, with its normal ups and downs. I reared four sons and lost one of them, which I will soon share with you.

I want to share this poem with you:

I'D PICK MORE DAISIES

If I had my life to live over again, I'd try to make more mistakes next time.

I would relax; I would limber up; I would be sillier than I have been this trip. I know of very few things I would take seriously. I would take more trips, climb more mountains, swim more rivers and watch more sunsets. I would do more walking and more looking. I would eat more ice cream and less beans. I would have more actual troubles and fewer imaginary ones.

You see, I am one of those people who live prophylactically and sensibly and sanely hour after hour, day after day, Oh, I've had moments and if I had it to do over again I would have more of them. In fact, I'd try to have nothing else—just moments—one after another instead of living so many years ahead each day.

I've been one of those people who never go anywhere without a thermometer, the hot water bottle, a gargle, a raincoat, an aspirin, or a parachute.

If I had it to do over again, I would go places and do things, and travel lighter than I have.

If I had my life to live over, I would start barefooted earlier in the spring and stay that way until later in the fall.

I would play hooky more. I wouldn't make such
good grades, except by accident. I would ride on more
merry-go-rounds and I'd pick more daisies.

That is the essence of my life.

I have been director of a counseling center in Atlanta,
Georgia for 10 years. I helped start this center because I
was interested in young people. The center was an out-
growth of the drug crisis and runaways in 1971. In Atlanta
there were many kids who ran away from home, and there
was a lot of concern about drugs. The community center
is a private, nonprofit counseling center where I started
as a volunteer. Though I had no training in the field of
counseling I was interested in young people. My husband
and I had a church group where adolescents came into
our home on a Sunday night. As our kids became teenagers
we decided to let go of the church and spend more time
with our own teenagers.

The first time I failed was when I got a speeding ticket.
As I was driving the car-pool for one of my youngest children, I heard a siren and saw a flashing light. The policeman pulled over behind me and there I was, right in front
of the elementary school which three of my kids attended.
Soon five hundred little heads popped to the windows and
all pointed at the lady who was being given a ticket. When
my boys came home, they said, "Mom, was that really you
being arrested outside school?"

That was a good experience for me because my driver's
license was taken away for speeding. Since I was driving
two Little League car-pools, I rented a horse and buggy.
After 2 weeks the authorities decided that I was a menace
on the streets, so they returned my license.

Losing my license was a leveling experience because I
was trying to set a good example and be a good model for
my kids—to be a "good mother." I discovered that one of

the most important things in mothering is to be a real person, though imperfect, because we can't live with perfection. If I were a perfect mother it would be very difficult for my kids to live up to that standard because they obviously are not perfect. If I were giving the impression that I was a perfect person who didn't make mistakes, that would be very hard for them to live up to. Their standards and their perfectionist orientation become too demanding.

As it turned out, I decided to get some training in the counseling center that we were developing. After 2 years of training as a volunteer with families and teaching youngsters to make choices and take the responsibility and consequences of their own actions, I returned to school at Georgia State University to be trained as a therapist and as a counselor. Very shortly I realized that one of the things I had to offer was my interest and caring about young people. Later they offered me the position of director of the center. My family urged me to accept, which I did.

One day in 1977, after returning from the grocery store, I found people standing in my carport and in the driveway looking in the back of a truck. As I drove into the driveway a neighbor came to my door and said, "We have to go to the hospital." The feeling in the pit of my stomach tightened. I said "Who?" He said, "Mitch." I said, "Motorcycle?" He was twenty and had a motorcyle. He said, "No, worse." We rushed to the hospital and when we got there my husband and older son, who was twenty-two, came out immediately and said, "It's too late, he's dead."

My instinct told me that I had to see him. I knew nothing about death—I had never even lost a parent, only one grandparent. But I knew instinctively that I needed to see him. People protected me, as is typical. They were telling me not to look because I'd be hurt too much. I learned that I needed to face it, I needed to look, I needed to see, I needed to touch, I needed to experience so that

I would not be able to deny, I would not be able to think my son was in Florida or in New York, and he'll be back soon.

I went straight to the door of his room. He was lying on a table. He had shot himself with two guns, once in the temple and once in the mouth while talking to his girlfriend on the telephone. She had broken up with him 3 weeks before. We knew he was depressed but we thought it was only due to the breakup. We only knew of one girlfriend but apparently there were four. Three of them he had promised to marry.

He had gotten a new job working at a big department store in Atlanta. He had started that job the week before. He hated the job, because he was a musician—creative, sensitive, talented, charming, attractive; he wanted to be a star, and he was a perfectionist. He had not learned how to fail, and he did not know how to succeed. He had signed a recording contract to do an album of his own music. But he said to one of the girlfriends, "How do I succeed and top this, or even match this?"

A week prior to his death he was really down about the girlfriend. When he began to play the piano, tears started streaming down his face. I put my arms around him and said, "It really hurts, doesn't it." And he said, "Yeah," and couldn't talk. But I just kind of held him and he played his music. Little did I know his pain was deeper than a lost love.

Then he started to talk. Two hours went by, and then three. We were talking about life and love, girlfriends and sex and relationships, school, careers, success and failure. I said, "You know, if this is success and this is failure, it takes both to make a whole," because I knew he struggled with success and failure. I knew he was a perfectionist, so we talked about how it's not the failure that counts—it's what we learn from the failure that's important.

From the time he was in kindergarten he always had a girlfriend; the girls would fight to sit next to him in kindergarten and kiss him—and he loved it.

During his final period of acute depression, I said, "since you've always had those relationships and now that you've broken up with your girlfriend, maybe you could take a look at what you want for yourself because you've always spent energy on the relationship rather than on yourself." I told him about some things he might do to get out of his depression. He did not respond but masked his depression. Many young people have depressions that are masked, and many which are overt and easier to spot. In the suicide prevention work I'm doing, I use a list of signs that one looks for, but they are not always apparent.

Looking back, I remember that there were a few signs. If I knew then what I know now, I might have had a chance to do something differently. I just have to say that I did what I had to do and he didn't hear me. He chose not to hear me.

On that Saturday morning I had gone to a meeting. My husband was home with the other two younger boys, fourteen and sixteen. Mitch was twenty, my oldest was twenty-two and married. Our cleaning lady was there, and the house was full of activity. I was the only person not there. Mitch received a call from the store where he worked saying that he was late. He said, "No, I'm not supposed to be there until 1 o'clock." They said, "No, that's next Saturday." He had mixed it up. He called his girlfriend and said, "I've blown my job. I'm gonna get fired. There's no point— I can't hack it. Who is the most important person in your life?" She said, "Well, I am. I have to say I am the most important person in my life." Thereupon he said, "I can't live with that. I will be a star in the sky and watch over you." At that point, while on the phone, he took the two guns and shot himself. My husband ran in and found my son, barely alive. He called for an ambulance and the police. The girlfriend came over and they were rushed to the hospital. The cleaning lady decided it was best that I should not see my son's bloody mattress, so they put it into a truck that had backed up into the carport and took it to the dump.

Looking back, that was the part that gave me the hardest time. I could face the things I saw — the things I experienced — but I had the hardest time facing the things I could not see or was not allowed to. The cleaning lady also closed Mitch's room and put a sign on the door that said Do Not Enter, and she signed her name. She thought that was the loving thing to do, to protect me from facing the horror. But when I came home and saw the sign, I realized that if I didn't go into that room then, I might never go in and that would make the room into a shrine.

I'd never had any grief training; I knew nothing about the process of grief, of mourning, of losing a loved one. I guess I thought I was immortal and so were my children. *friends*. I really had never thought about death, though I expected to bury my parents, but not my children or a child.

The shock that I experienced at first was a kind of numbness. It came after I went into the hospital room where my son lay. I had to look at him. He was naked but covered with a white cloth and I needed to touch him — I needed to take off his bracelet. He was breathing, because he was on a machine. I told the nurse he was alive, but she said no. The machine was keeping his kidneys alive so that they could be given to someone. It seemed impossible to accept the fact that he was dead because he was breathing. They asked us to leave the room so they could do what they needed to do. I remember needing to leave the room on my own terms. They said that I would have to leave now and started to take me by the elbow. It was very important for me to not let people guide me by the elbow. Everybody was doing this with me, as if I were disabled. I *was* disabled, but I was not an invalid. It was important for me to decide when to leave the room. I told them I would leave when I was ready to leave.

I finished touching him, and took off his bracelet. That bracelet was very important to me and still is. I did not cry. I was too numb, in shock. I could not believe it—it was just unbelievable. I had no preparation. I knew only that he was sad about breaking up with his girlfriend, no more than that.

At the hospital I was so shocked that I could not respond emotionally. It was just like moving in a dream—slow motion. We left the room and went home. People were calling and the house began to fill with visitors. I was still numb. I could not think. Phones began to ring, people began to answer the phones. People were coming into the house, some bringing food, crying. My mind kept saying that suicide just couldn't happen in my family. I had never known anyone who had committed suicide. So the stigma struck all of a sudden. We were a well-respected family. My first feeling was: I have failed my son; I have failed myself; I have failed my family; and I have failed the center that I directed. The burden of those failures was almost unbearable.

Question: You said something before about the mattress being taken away from the house before you could see it. Why was that important?

Answer: That's the part I had the worst time accepting because I couldn't see the mattress. I wanted to know all about the mattress, and I had to hear over and over what it looked like. Again and again I asked my husband to tell me. Two years later one of my sons told me that the worst part of it for him was the odor. That helped me. It may sound strange, but it helped me. My hus-

band probably would not have had the nerve or
the courage to tell me in order to protect me.
But it was important for my son to share that
with me.

Prior to Mitch's suicide, as part of my training for counseling, I had gone through a number of psychiatric sessions
with an Atlanta therapist. He was among the first persons
to come to us after the event. He told us that there was a
gift in his death if we looked for it, "but you'll have to look.
It won't jump out at you." These were very important words
for me to hear. It meant that somehow there was hope;
that some day maybe I'd find meaning in his death.

My husband's reaction was different. He said he heard
the words but they had no meaning for him. His candor
was very important because I wanted to accept his grieving
and his feelings as different from mine—not right or
wrong, but different. So he grieved by being strong and
private and holding up for me and the family, and I accepted that. It is not that he wasn't hurting but that he was
grieving differently and felt he needed to be strong for
everyone. Often when my mind was up, his was down, and
vice versa. And that was very helpful to both of us.

Another thing my therapist recommended was to use
this time of crisis to bring our family together in a way that
nothing else could ever do. He said, "if you have 50 people
in your home and there is a decision to be made such as
cremation or not, who the pallbearers are going to be, call
the family together and have a private family conference.
Never close the door to the children, no matter how old,
because behind closed doors scary things can be imagined.
Always include the children."

Our children weren't that young. The youngest was
fourteen. In our first conference we also included the
girlfriend who was on the telephone at the time. In our

inclusion of each other there was a camaraderie and a closeness that may be difficult to understand. We gathered the
family together in the bedroom and the question at hand
was discussed. Everybody was able to give an opinion.

We did not build a shrine for Mitch, but we kept our
memories balanced. Instead of saying only wonderful
things about him, one of my boys was able to say, "I'll never
forget the night that Mitch and I played tennis at midnight
in the park, about a mile away, and I beat the pants off of
him. He was so mad at me that he made me walk home in
the dark at 1 o'clock in the morning." That was okay. It
was real, it wasn't phony. It wasn't "He was so wonderful—
he was so this, he was so beautiful." He was, and we talked
about that, too. But we also talked about the reality of who
Mitch was.

We never built a shrine; we never put him on a pedes-
tal, which is easy to do to a dead child. It's easy to remember
only the good things and to forget the bad parts. Mitch
was sunshine and tears.—He could walk into a room and
pick a fight and then walk out. He was selfish and yet he
would give you the shirt off his back. He was kind and
loving, and if there was a little puppy that was hurt he
would bring it home.

Mitch was very sensitive, probably too sensitive for this
world. He couldn't handle injustice, especially when
teachers would be cruel to other kids or cruel to him. He
had a learning disability as a youngerster. Children who
have learning disabilities, or children who are gifted, are
very susceptible to suicidal thoughts perhaps because they
are labeled, set apart, or feel different.

During the next few days family sessions were called
regularly. I learned that my son's death gave life a value
and meaning that I had never felt before. I had enjoyed
my kids; I played with them; I laughed with them and cried
with them, and I'd look at them, but I'm not really sure

that I always saw them. There is a difference between looking at someone and looking deeply into the other person and seeing who is really there.

About 3 weeks after my son's death, my two sons and my husband and I went out for dinner. All of a sudden my family came into crystal-clear focus. I could see each one of them and I thought, what a beautiful moment; my healing already had begun.

✳ Probably my hardest struggle was with my guilt. I thought I had failed Mitch in some way; that I had done things that I shouldn't have done, and I should have done what I had left undone. Even though I knew I had been a "good mother," I berated myself and felt guilty. I learned later that I needed to feel guilty until I got tired. I finally decided I am still me; I have the same values, the same morals, the same principles I've always had. I'm no different in the sense of who I am; but I'll never be the same. I will never be the same person I was before that day. A part of me had been destroyed but I'm still me and I have the same morals and principles. So I had to decide what to do with the remainder of my life. ✳

For years I had been working with families trying to help them let their kids make decisions and choices about their life and let them be responsible for the consequences. Now I asked myself, "could I do that myself?" This was the ultimate test for me.

> Question: Did you have a viewing? a traditional funeral? We had a death in our family. My niece's child was killed by a bus and my husband made a decision not to view the body, and it was a very bad experience for the whole family.
>
> Answer: I think that people who do grief work and teach the process of mourning recommend that you look at the body so that you don't

deny the death, because denial is very detrimental. But, it's an individual matter; what is right for one may not be right for another. Sometimes when grief goes on and on it becomes a life-style. Another therapist in town who was working with a couple called me in as a consultant because it had been 4 or 5 years since their child died and they were continuing to brood, particularly the mother. It was a way of life. Their friends were leaving them because that was all they talked about. It was an obsession. After working with them for a while I said, "How old would your child be when he would probably have left your home?" She said, "He probably would have been on his own at around twenty-one." I asked, "When would your son have been twenty-one?" "It would be," she said, "in another 8 months." I said, "Could you mourn and really grieve for another 8 months until your son is twenty-one, and on his twenty-first birthday release him and let him go as you would have in life?" They agreed they could do that, and so they grieved and mourned for 8 more months, and then had a big celebration at the twenty-first birthday. Their grief was a mind set. When they him let go, it was as though he was out on his own in the world. After the party, they resumed a much more normal life. They're different; they'll never be the same, but they can go on. They made a choice.

⚓ There comes a point when you choose to live or die and that's what happened to me. I wanted to die. The pain was too bad. Someone said this morning that a person never really wants to die, but they can't stand the pain of living as they perceive it. I believe that is a true statement. That is what I was experiencing. I could then see how my son could be in such pain and agony that he could choose death over the life and the pain that he had experienced. People gave me alcohol: "Don't hurt, Iris; have a drink—you'll feel better." I didn't need to feel better. I needed to hurt. I needed to go through the pain to get beyond it. It was a choice; there came a day when I finally had to decide whether I was going to live or die.✶

✶A therapist said to me at the funeral, "You may need to get angry with your son, and if you do and want someone with you I'm available; if you need to do that alone, I respect that." I thought at the time—get angry at my dead son? You're crazy! But the seed was planted. I needed to do it alone, and I was ultimately able to go to the cemetery and stamp on his grave and scream and wail and curse him, God, and me, the world, and get it out of me.✶

Three nights after my son's death I awoke and threw up. That was something I had never experienced—an emotional trauma bad enough to cause vomiting. Then I heard poetry. I literally heard poetry. My son had a book by Thomas Hardy open on his bed. He had underlined passages that death by suicide is the ultimate release from loneliness, depression, and pain. There was a lot of poetry that he had also underlined where Hardy's characters had ended their own lives. In high school Mitch had written a paper on that subject.

I woke up hearing poetry and it was an incredible experience. My husband was asleep for the first time in 3 nights. I didn't want to move and yet I thought if I don't write this down I'll lose it. I couldn't see, it was pitch dark. So I got out of bed, which woke him up, and went into the den and started to write. The words kept coming and coming; it was a sense of giving birth and vomiting at the same time.

Three hours later I went back to bed and fell asleep.

Then I awoke and went to take a bath. As I bathed I heard music that Mitch had recorded and left on a tape recorder. We learned later that he had played this piece of music and sung the words to all four girlfriends. One by one he had taken them to the church which has a large grand piano, and played the song and sung the words to each of them, and said that he had written it just for them. In a sense I'm sure he did. I had never heard the music; but on this morning it came from my sixteen-year-old son's room, which was underneath the bathroom. It was just gorgeous music. When I realized what music it was, four more verses in the poem came to mind that were about his music. I realized I hadn't written a word about his music the night before. My father, a writer, took those verses and added them in the poem. The story of the poem was healing for me. Some mourners write music, some paint, some people write poetry, some people write letters to the dead child or spouse. Whatever works for you, I learned, is the kind of thing to use.

> Question: I just wondered what other charac-
> teristics of your son could you look back upon
> and see a kind of danger sign; and also, what was
> the meaning of his involvement with girls? How
> do you explain that part of his personality?
>   Answer: I think his ego needed to be stroked.
> He was very attractive, charming, and talented,
> but he always undervalued himself because he
> had a learning disability and because kids teased
> him in school as a slow learner. He was the one
> who would sit and look out the window for 20
> minutes and then have to stay after school to do
> the work he hadn't done in those 20 minutes.
> Other kids thought he was dumb, so he thought
> he was dumb. Actually he had an I.Q. of 145 but

for a long time he didn't believe he was smart. We provided professional help for his learning disability, along with the special schools. We tried to show him that his potential was real and that his learning disability was perceptual. There wasn't anything wrong with him except for the particular perceptual difficulty. He also played the drums, had a band, performed in schools, sang in a quartet, was the champion tennis player and champion ping-pong player.

I think the girlfriends were an ego need. Their adulations told him that he was really worth something, that he was a young man of great talent and promise.

✴ You asked about danger signs. I think there were some signs such as the card he left on the breakfast table one morning. I didn't pick up the sign probably because I didn't know there were signs to look for, and it never occurred to me that anybody I knew would commit suicide. But there was the card from Mitch a few days after he had broken up with his last girlfriend. It said, "To Mom and Dad. Thanks for making a lot of hell a little bit of heaven." I thought it referred to the breakup with a girlfriend, but it was more than that.

Looking back, I recall the night he bought ice cream for everybody. Earlier that day he had gone to a drug store and charged boxes of candy, Valentines Day cards and all kinds of gifts for these girlfriends. Then he took them one by one to a trysting place and presented his Valentine. It was his way of saying goodbye. When he came home he brought ice cream for everyone in the house. It was the night before he died. There was a look about his eyes that last night; he had never bought ice cream for the family. Surely that was a sign right there. He didn't spend much money because he didn't have much. For him to have brought ice cream home for the whole family was a sign that I might pick up today. It was peaceful, it was wonderful. Everybody was loving and having a marvelous time—but he looked strange. I followed him to his room and said, "Are you okay?" And he said, "Well, no worse than any other night." Again I assumed his sadness was due to the girlfriend matter, and to the pain of being rejected.

One of the guns he used had been kept by one of his girlfriends for about a year. When he asked for it back, she was scared. She didn't know whether to tell us or not.

Question: I was wondering, in terms of your healing process, was there a certain kind of guilt in the healing itself as when people looked at you when you smiled and thought that you really were not taking it seriously? After all, how could you be smiling only 3 months after what happened!

Answer: No, I never felt that, but I had an obsession to talk about it; I had to tell the world. For example, when I went to get a watchband repaired at the jeweler I found myself telling the jeweler. It didn't make sense but I had this need to tell it and tell it until I was finished telling it. I also felt the world knew because we are fairly well-known in the community. The news had been on the radio, on television, all over the high school. I had the feeling that when I drove my car down the street there was a sign on it that said, *My son killed himself*. I just knew that every-

body knew. As cars came and passed I remember
thinking—"well, they know now." This was totally irrational.

The world expects you to heal very quickly. They do
not want you to talk about it; they don't want you to mention
his name for fear that if you're crying you'll fall apart and
then they won't know how to handle you. If your friends
have kids of the same age, some may really try to avoid
you. For a hundred reasons friends may run from you,
hoping they can pick up the relationship when things have
settled down. But they don't settle down, not for a long
time. It will take about a year, you tell yourself, and then
it's terrible all over again because it is an anniversary. All
such firsts are important. Some experts say it takes at least
2 years, depending on the kind of help you had. I had
therapy twice a week and then every week for two and a
half to three years. Then I went once a month. I was pushed
through the stages; I was pushed to feel guilty and to be
angry, but I was nurtured at the same time. That was rare,
and I am eternally grateful.

When it first happened I had a dream that I was a
can of salmon floating in space—that something had burst
out from the can's inside and there were jagged edges all
around. My body was the can but I was also out floating
free. After a while I came in and looked inside the can
and saw that it was metallic and empty. Three weeks later,
after I'd made my decision to survive, I had the same dream
again. But this time I looked into the can and saw an organ,
a pink membrane, and I woke up knowing I would survive.

Once I had made my choice to survive, I told my
therapist, "I don't know what to do. Some people are
suggesting that I go away for 6 months and heal myself
and then come back to work. What should I do?"

He said, "Well, what do you want to do?" And I said,

"I really think I want to go back to work after we spend a week in Florida." He said, "Why don't you do that?" "Well, you know," I said, "my staff doesn't meet until Monday and this is Thursday, and we are leaving on Saturday, and . . ." He said, "Are you the director?" And I said, "Yes, but . . ." He said, "Are you the director or not?" And I thought, yes, I'm the director. I went out of his office, telephoned my secretary, and said, "I want you to call a staff meeting and I want everybody there." She said, "Yes, ma'am." It was the first and last time she's ever "yes, ma'am'd" me. That felt good; finally I was able to take charge. That was the real beginning of my healing.

We went to Florida, but when we came back I was still struggling with the possibility that because of the suicide in my family my counseling center might be incapable of delivering good work. How could I hope to be effective as a counselor when I had not been able to prevent a suicide in my own family? That thought was a heavy burden.

What actually happened was close to a miracle. Other parents who had lost a child came to me, referred by friends and acquaintances who had read of our tragedy. In one case, a local boy was killed in a car accident and our family was able to go at once to the hospital. Soon, the father was sobbing out his grief in the arms of one of my sons. The episode gave a new meaning to my own bereavement and my future. Immediately, I was struck by what I had been told in the very beginning, that Mitch's death might somehow be turned into a gift.

Soon, my circle of bereaved parents grew larger. Doctors and lawyers began sending us their clients who had lost children through suicide, accidental death, or murder. I was deeply grateful for their faith that we could be of help. A fellow professional offered a reason. He said, "It's because they know you won't judge them as parents. They know you have expertise which they lack but they also know that you are a parent who has survived a suicide, and that you have learned something important because of that experience."

He was right. I had learned, and I have continued to learn. Soon, I was attending Emory University. There, I was allowed to major in suicidology, the only student in the entire university majoring in that subject. Since then, I've been developing my own curriculum, one course a quarter. As a full-time director of my center, we must raise money to keep our doors open. Whenever funding gets low, I take an Incomplete in my course, raise some more money, and get the center's payroll going again. Then, I go back and finish my Incomplete. As of now, I've finished my course work for a Master's degree. Oral examinations are scheduled for May, and I'll do my thesis this summer, which perhaps will culminate in a book on suicidology, prevention, intervention and postvention. That makes meaning out of the meaninglessness of my son's death.

Question: There's one other person involved here that I'm curious to know about. Since I'm a man, and involved in this thing, I can identify with your husband when he told you not to go into that room. We are told to be the protectors. How did he get through it? You had your work and you had people coming to you. But what did he do?

Answer: My husband is very outgoing, very gregarious, very funny, and laughs a lot. We sing together and we have a lot of fun. I think he felt that he needed to be strong in order to protect me. All through the funeral he was protecting me. Afterwards, he let me do what I needed to do. We held each other at night, we clung to each other. One makes a choice—either you blame each other or you come closer together. Eighty-five percent of the married couples who lose a child get divorced after their loss because they feel they must blame somebody. We didn't need to blame each other, because we let Mitch bear the responsibility for his decision. My husband talked only a little to me about his pain and his agony, and he shed most of his tears privately. I respected that. I know that he shared with our oldest son because they grieved in the same way. He felt some anger and probably some guilt. He also had his work in advertising and a hobby as a "ham" at amateur radio.

Our family conferences helped because we could talk about Mitch and not build a shrine to him. I think we have found a balance. Mitch was a sunshine and tears young man. If there is thunder, someone might say, "Well, Mitch is riding his motorcycle in heaven again." It's comforting, I think, if you can jest about that after 4 years of healing. My husband is healing. He did not choose the initial outlet of talking as much as I did. His talking was more selective. In the work that I do with couples I keep saying, "You may need to do your healing differently." I needed to talk and talk and talk.

At this point my husband and I are able to talk freely. We have a kind of balance. I think we have accepted the fact of Mitch's death. We don't like it, but we realize that we don't have to like it! We don't understand it, but we don't have to understand it. What we do have to do is to make a choice about our lives. The choice we have made it to survive and find meaning in our lives because of Mitch's death. We now value each other, our family, friends, and life in a way that we never did before. In the words of a favorite aunt:

These days are the Winter of the soul.
But Spring comes and brings new life and beauty
Because of the growth of the roots in the dark.

Chapter 14

FIRST-LINE HELP
FOLLOWING A FUNERAL

Earl A. Grollman

The cry for help goes unheeded. A person kills himself or herself, life is over.

For the family, tragedy is just beginning. There is just not enough time to heal the wounds of a self-inflicted death. The crushing blow is a bitter experience for all those left behind. They carry it in their hearts for the rest of their lives.

The death of a loved one is devastating. Yet the bereaved may find consolation in believing that it was God's will, or in accepting the reality factor that there are limits to one's existence. How much more traumatic when loss of life is self-willed! Where do the survivors find consolation then? Suicide is the cruelest death of all for those who remain.

The "unpardonable sin" has been committed; the universal taboo with its theological imprimatur has been degradingly violated. Some say piously: "Suicide is self-murder. It is against the Sixth Commandment and the worst crime of all." Inwardly they hold the family and close friends partially or wholly accountable for the transgression.

For the relatives and friends, intolerable feelings of guilt and grief are aroused. The widowed spouse will never know if some act of unkindness on his or her part was the spark that inflamed the mate with the urge for self-execution. Parents feel that they must have failed their child miserably and blame themselves for the negligence. And the children of a suicide go through life haunted by the fact that perhaps they did something to precipitate the parent's death. They may even believe that the cruel seed of self-destruction that destroyed their mother or father is lurking in themselves as well, that something is wrong with their psychological inheritance. There is the persistent, gnawing question, "What did I do wrong?"

Survivors carry the stigma for life. Years afterward, a woman is still remembered as "the one whose husband shot himself." Suicide is never completely forgotten and forgiven.

But someone has died and must be buried. No matter how difficult the situation, there are still ways to be of assistance to those who face the greatest tragedy and challenge of their lives.

The Funeral

It is understandable that when the survivors hear the shocking news their first impulse is to hold the funeral as quickly and quietly as possible. After all, there is an aura of shame and dishonor. As a result, a private service for the immediate family may be contemplated.

But no matter how great the humiliation, the relative

cannot hide from reality. Nor can one run away from pain. A private funeral seems to say that the family is unable to bear the disgrace before their friends and neighbors, and therefore want to keep it "secret." The family overlook one important fact—that when given the opportunity, friends may be of help with supportive love.

The funeral offers an important opportunity to comfort the mourners. It is the rite of separation. The "bad dream" is real. The presence of the corpse actualizes the experience. In this way, the process of denial can be transformed to the acceptance of reality.

In the eulogy, the clergy should avoid any reference to blasphemy. The person who took his/her life was still a person, with strengths as well as weaknesses. The positive aspects of that individual life should be mentioned so that people can recall the happy times and the many ways in which life was enriched by the remembered presence. After all, one judges a person by the total years, not by an isolated moment, cataclysmic as it may be.

Coming to Grips with Grief

The goals in ministering to the family of the suicide are similar to those in helping all who have suffered bereavement. In Erich Lindemann's words: "Grief work is emancipation from the bondage of the deceased, readjustment to the environment in which the deceased is missing, and the formation of new relationships."

In comforting the bereaved, one must take into account the *special kind* of death. What can care givers bring? Their best self—neither prejudiced by outmoded prohibitions, nor judgmental of the actions of the deceased or the survivors. They have not come either to justify or to censure; they have come, with caring undiminished, as care givers.

What about the guilt of the bereaved family?

The "living victims" are the survivors who bear the burden of guilt and the stigma of having loved one who has willfully taken his or her life. The widowed spouse may feel responsible for inciting the mate's act of self-execution. Parent's blame themselves for insensitivity, and the children of a suicide are haunted by the fact that they perhaps could have prevented their parent's death.

It is of no help to say, "Don't talk about it." The bereaved is going through an intense emotional crisis and needs to articulate and act out reactions—loud denial, turning slowly to bewilderment, and finally to weeping, despairing confrontation with the truth of the loss. Review the memories of the deceased, and as pain is felt at the recall of these experiences, the individual begins slowly to dissolve the emotional burden. Interest should be genuine and sincere. One should not try too hard. Oversolicitation only engenders further suspicions and guilt. Listen responsively to what the other experiences from his or her internal agonizing frame of reference. Although suicide is often viewed as insane behavior, to inform the family that the person who killed him or herself was crazy only brings fear of inherited mental illness.

How can you tell if the survivor's reactions are unusual?

In general, one is able to distinguish normal from pathological grief not by the latter's being abnormal *per se*, but rather by emotional reactions being so intense and prolonged that the physical and mental well-being are jeopardized.

When grief work is not done, the survivor may suffer morbid distress characterized by delayed responses. He or she may show great fortitude at the funeral but later develop symptoms of agitated depression and bodily affliction. This bereaved may complain of such psychosomatic illnesses as ulcerative colitis, rheumatoid arthritis, asthma, and hypochondriasis (imaginary ills). Symptoms of a tension headache may lead to the conclusion by the bereaved that he or she has a brain tumor; arthritic pain is interpreted as heart disease; constipation becomes a symptom of malignancy. Obsessive-compulsive behavior may manifest itself. One may try to appease guilt through extreme cleanliness. Or one may be unwilling to terminate the atmosphere of the funeral service. i.e., "Tell me the eulogy again." There may be self-destructive behavior detrimental to social and economic existence. If there are any doubts as to one's emotional health, professional help should be consulted.

A final note

Now that the funeral is over, you start slowly to bring the survivors to some degree of purpose. In Hebrew there is a word, *T'shuvah*. It means "to relive" and implies the opportunity of a renewed attempt, a fresh start, and even a new beginning. *T'shuvah* insists that the past need not continue to haunt, that one can use the past as a spiritual springboard for change and growth, and that the scars of tragedy can be healed.

SUGGESTED READINGS

Bibliography on suicide and suicide prevention . 1897-1957, 1958-1967. Chevy Chase: National Institute of Mental Health, 1969.

Blaine, G.B., Jr. *Youth and the hazards of affluence.* New York: Harper & Row, 1966.

Dublin, L. *Suicide: A sociological and statistical study.* New York: Ronald Press, 1963.

Durkheim, E. *Suicide, a study in sociology.* Ill.: Free Press, 1951.

Ellis, E.R., & Allen, G.N. *Within our suicide problem.* New York: Doubleday, 1961.

Farber, M.L. *Theory of suicide.* New York: Funk & Wagnalls, 1968.

Farberow, N.L. & Schneidman, E.S. (Eds.). *The cry for help.* New York: McGraw-Hill, 1961.

Fretzel, P.W. *Understanding the suicidal person.* Nashville: Abingdon Press, 1972.

Freud, S. *Civilization and its discontents.* (J. Strachey, Ed. and trans.) New York: W.W. Norton, 1962. (Originally published, 1930).

————. Mourning and melancholia. *Collected Papers,* (Vol. IV). (J. Strachey, Ed. and trans.) London: The Hogarth Press, 1949.

Grollman, E.A. *Suicide: Prevention, intervention, postvention.* Boston: Beacon Press, 1971.

Henry, F., & Short, J.F., Jr. *Suicide and homicide.* Glencoe, Ill.: Free Press, 1954.

Kiev, A. *The early recognition and treatment of potentially suicidal persons.* New York: Behavioral Publications, 1971.

Meerloo, J.A.M. *Suicide and mass suicide.* New York: Grune & Stratton, 1962.

Menninger, K.A. *Man against himself.* New York: Harcourt, Brace, 1938.

Oates, W.E. *Where to go for help.* Philadelphia: The Westminster Press, 1972.

Resnik, H.L.P. Center comments. *Bulletin of Suicidology,* National Institute of Mental Health, Spring, 1970.

————. (Ed.) *The diagnosis and management of the suicidal individual.* Boston: Little, Brown & Company, 1967.

————. & Cantor, J.M. Suicide and aging. *Journal of the American Geriatric Society,* February 1970.

Richman, J. & Rosenbaum, M. The family doctor and the suicidal family. *Psychiatry in Medicine,* January 1970.

St. John-Stevas, N. *Life, death and the law.* Bloomington: Indiana University Press, 1961.

Schneidman, E.S. (Ed.) *Essays in self-destruction*. New York: International Science Press, 1967.

————, & Farberow, N.L. *Clues to suicide*. New York: McGraw-Hill, 1957.

————, & Mandelkorn, P. *How to prevent suicide*. Public Affairs Pamphlet No. 406, 1967.

Seiden, R.H. *Campus tragedy: A study of student suicide*. Grant #5T, HG-8104, National Institute of Mental Health.

Sprott, S.E. *The English debate on suicide*. LaSalle, Ill.: Open Court Publishing Company, 1961.

Stengel, E. *Suicide and attempted suicide*. Baltimore: Penguin Books, 1964.

Teicher, J.D. Why adolescents kill themselves. *National Health Program Reports*, January 1970.

Williams, G. *The sanctity of life*. New York: Knopf, 1957.

Chapter 15

INTERVENTION BY THE PASTORAL COUNSELOR WITH SURVIVORS OF A SUICIDE

Jacob Goldberg

Pastoral Bereavement Counseling may be defined as counseling for mourners provided by clergypersons, directed toward a specific goal, and operating through a structured sequence. Such counseling may be particularly useful in the special circumstances of counseling the survivors of a suicide. The pastoral counselor should also be aware of the unique factors that may arise in such a situation.

The clergyperson who has undertaken special training to enable him or her to minister to bereaved persons has a unique role advantage in dealing with suicide survivors. He or she is often perceived as the "shepherd of the flock," as a caring and loving personality, as one whose empathy can radiate in a helpful and healthy manner. If the clergy-counselor will seek to transmit, within the therapeutic encounter, this feeling of "understanding another's pain," of a non-judgmental acceptance of sorrow, anger, and guilt, and of an unquestioned recognition of the mourner's basic worth and dignity—despite the indignity of the connection with someone whose actions have embarrassed them—the clergy-counselor will have helped a great deal.

Just because society looks somewhat askance at the aberration of suicide, and just because many people feel a greater degree of discomfort than in confronting an "ordinary death," grief therapy by a pastoral counselor may be uniquely beneficial. It places a community-sanctioned figure of authority in a potentially effective position to enhance the mourner's sense of self-worth. Pastoral Bereavement Counseling can provide a means for more than just ventilation of painful feelings, although this is extremely valuable in itself. Through Pastoral Bereavement Counseling the mourner can receive support and emotional buttressment to alleviate self-accusations regardiong his or her own role in the suicide situation.

Often, the survivor of a suicide will experience more intensely the anger and guilt than is normal in the bereavement process. Whether it is guilt at their acts of commission or omission in the events leading up to the suicide, or anger at the deceased, the special circumstances color their feelings with greater poignancy and compulsion. The irrevocable aspect of both the death and the manner of death places an additional burden of psychological adjustment upon the mourner. The pastoral counselor must be prepared to deal with the special pain that will be confronted. Empathy, support, endurance, and acceptance—these are the therapeutic modes that the pastoral bereavement counselor employs in interactions with the mourner. The goal is strictly limited—to support the mourner in the first steps toward adjustment to the reality of loss by suicide. Pastoral Bereavement Counseling is not open-ended; it has a limited time span and focuses on specific targets. It is designed to minimize the possible arousal of transference and to prevent feelings of dependence upon the counselor.

Pastoral Bereavement Counseling for the survivors of a suicide requires a greater therapeutic intensity than Pastoral Bereavement Counseling in general, in response to the more intense trauma of bereavement after a suicide. The clergy-counselor is also in a position to "work through" some of the spiritual ambivalence and confusion that may arise in these special circumstances. The normal "anger against God," which in normal bereavement can be seen as a healthy specification and labelling of an otherwise "free-flowing" pain (and which the pastoral counselor can help resolve through counseling) cannot be faced as clearly in the case of a suicide. Some of the psycho-religious issues that may need to be faced are, "Was it a human act, for which God is not responsible?" Or, "Is God responsible for the overwhelming pressures that drove the deceased to the act of taking his (or her) own life?"

The pastoral counselor should aim to help the mourner sort out his or her feelings, to become more clearly aware of the combination of emotion and religion that is inherent in the mourning process. Through therapy, the mourner-survivor can be helped to perceive inner confusion, sorrow, religious doubts, and personal philosophy, as an essentially healthy stage in coming to face the reality of sorrow. In such cases the pastoral counselor can facilitate the mourner returning to "peace with his (or her) God," through a therapeutically valid and emotionally healthy process.

Related to this task is also the search for restoring a sense of the basic meaning of life and the worthiness of struggle, to replace the sense of tragedy and waste that arise after a suicide. In these and other aspects of counseling in this special situation, the pastoral counselor can serve a unique function in moving the survivor towards a healthy "resolution of grief."

Part III

SPECIAL ASPECTS
OF SUICIDE

INTRODUCTION

This section has been designated *Special Aspects of Suicide* because the two chapters it comprises do not belong in the first two sections owing to their particular subject matter. They offer perspectives on suicide that are not readily considered in the study of prevention and bereavement.

Chapter 16, *Anthropological Perspectives on Suicide*, categorizes suicide as an activity that is culturally evaluated, that occurs within a framework of social relationships. There is no single general cause, it takes different forms, and it evokes diverse cultural attitudes. Primitive societies vary as widely as modern societies in the frequency, mode, causes, and explanation of suicide. Therefore, it is risky to make crosscultural comparisons. The author, however, does find some parallels between types, forms, and effects of African suicide and our own culture; in both, suicide may be caused by the conflict in or inability to perform domestic roles, and failure in status hierarchy.

Chapter 17, *Self-Destructive Behavior—Slow Dying* cites alcoholism and drug abuse as major examples of slow suicide. The diabetic who refuses insulin and others who do not comply with medical management are also committing slow suicide when looked at from a psychodynamic point of view. Slow dying afflicts those who are incapable of controlling their disease, such as paralysis victims, and people with chronically debilitating diseases which will slowly destroy their body. The task of the therapist and the treatment team is the practical management of the disease by developing systems to help the patient to maintain a modicum of mastery over bodily functions. Words of support in such situations are empty. The author also draws attention to the psychological and emotional drain on the staff, and suggests the need for staff supports in their helping efforts. He reminds us that professionals in this field have to face questions of morality, ethics, and religion, as for example, when the patient asks the professional to hasten death—the question of euthanasia. The professional first needs to put his or her own house in order regarding these issues.

Chapter 16

ANTHROPOLOGICAL PERSPECTIVES ON SUICIDE

Sydel Silverman

To understand the role of culture in the phenomenon of suicide, it is necessary to step back from our own moral convictions and consider the broad range of cultural variation in the incidence of suicide, its etiology, and the significance attached to it. Anthropology has long had an interest in the study of suicide because it can be diagnostic of fundamental cultural views of life and death, and diagnostic also of stress points in a social structure. Yet there have been very few studies that go beyond illustrative cases and virtually no systematic crosscultural comparison. What we do know is that the cultural factors in suicide are complex. The professional who deals with an ethnically diverse population needs to be alert to the variability, but he or she should not expect to find specific "cultural attitudes" attached to members of specific groups.

The base line of all social-science research on suicide

is Emile Durkheim's classic study (1975). His monumental contribution was to treat suicide as a social regularity, a "social fact" quite apart from the psychological and other processes that determine the specific individuals affected. Durkheim offered a typology of three kinds of suicide—altruistic, egoistic, and anomic—related to different kinds of social structures. His main focus was on "anomic" suicide, which he thought occurs in situations where social life is institutionalized but the institutions are inadequate to bind people to their purposes. The incidence of anomic suicide was for Durkheim an index of social disorganization. While this scheme still influences contemporary research, it has limited usefulness in throwing light on the anthropologist's case materials. For instance, suicide may result from the very success with which individuals have been integrated into the institution of their culture.

The specifically anthropological approach to suicide looks at it as an activity that is culturally evaluated and that occurs within a framework of social relationships. The point of departure for this approach was B. Malinowski's discussion of suicide in the Trobriand Islands, in his monograph *Crime and Custom in Savage Society* (1926). In one famous case, a sixteen-year-old boy has carried on a relationship culturally defined as incestuous, with his mother's sister's daughter. The incest was generally known and tolerated until a discarded lover of the girl made a scandal of it, threatening the culprit with black magic and then insulting him in public. The next morning the accused boy donned ceremonial attire and climbed to the top of a coconut palm, where he addressed the community about his misdeed and about the man who was now driving him to suicide; then he jumped 60 feet to his death. His clansmen were obliged to avenge him, and fights and quarrels followed. Malinowksi's point was to show the disparity between rules of conduct and the way sanctions are brought into effect in actual daily life, but he also showed how the transgression of a norm exposes the institution—the suicide in this case revealing the tensions in a system of matrilineal clans.

Another landmark anthropological discussion of suicide appeared in Ruth Benedict's *Pattern of Culture* (1934). Attitudes to suicide, Benedict noted in this tract on extreme cultural relativism, are as variable as attitudes to life and death.

> Suicide may be a light matter, the recourse of anyone who has suffered some slight rebuff, an act that occurs constantly in a tribe. It may be the highest and noblest act a wise man can perform. The very tale of it, on the other hand, may be a matter for incredulous mirth, and the act itself impossible to conceive as a human possibility. Or it may be a crime punishable by law, or regarded as a sin against the gods (p. 41).

Among the Plains Indians, suicide was institutionalized as a means of gaining status; a man could take a suicide pledge for a year, deliberately risking his life, and if he survived, he could claim public honors. The Zuñi Indians of the Southwest, on the other hand, could not conceive of suicide and smiled unbelievingly when told of cases among white men. For the Dobu Islanders off the coast of New Guinea, suicide could be used to win pity and the support of one's relatives, or it could express humiliation and malice when the ill will of the universe seems to have turned against one. Among the Kwakiutl of the American Northwest Coast, suicide was a means of wiping out shame when some grave insult had been suffered—as when a man stumbled in his initiation dance.

What do we know about suicide the world over? First, it is clear that there is no single general cause, and no straightforward correlations that can account for the incidence of suicide. Furthermore, we know that primitive societies can vary as widely as do record-keeping societies in the frequency, mode, causes, and explanations of suicide. We also know that making crosscultural comparisons is an extremely risky business. Even where statistics are available, the comparison of figures can be misleading. For instance, there are indications that the differences long noted in suicide rates among the different Scandinavian countries disappear if the figures on all unexpected deaths (including suicide, homicide, and accidents) are merged. Moreover, comparing suicide events in different cultures may be an artificial exercise if the cultural meanings attached are quite different.

Some well-known instances of the variability in cultural meanings will illustrate. Even among the superficially similar Scandinavian countries, there are profound differences in attitudes toward suicide. In Norway, it is apt to be regarded as sign of weakness and cowardice and as a sin against God. The Swedish view, in contrast, is generally tolerant and secularized, and the high rates of suicide appear to be related to needs for achievement and fears of dependence. In Finland, where there are rejecting attitudes toward deviance, suicide is virtually a taboo subject, and relatives of victims and survivors of suicide attempts are likely to react with denial.

The most extreme case of cultural attitudes conducive to suicide is probably Japan. The institutionalization of suicide is elaborate, and there are many situations under which the proper performance of one's social role would actually require suicide. There is a vast vocabulary for the types of institutionalized suicide that differ by method, forms of ritualization, motive, and so on, reflecting the many kinds of suicide that are given explicit cultural recognition. In addition, the rates of noninstitutionalized suicide are high. the psychological dynamics seem to be related to a strong consciousness of status differences (allowing little means of expressing resentment), intense emphasis upon success, and what George DeVos has called "role narcissism"—the complete identification with social role. Moreover, Buddhist concepts of life and death rationalize an escape from life through suicide biological life is but the temporary lodging of the soul, and the realization of the true self is in disavowing attachments to worldly things, and ultimately, in the negation of biological life.

Some excellent comparative studies of suicide among American Indians point up the very different patterns that may account for suicide and thus the perils of comparing actual suicide rates. The American Indian material also shows the different effects that reservation life had on suicide patterns in different groups. In some instances, as among the Shoshone, Pima, Papago, and Yaqui, the reservation period brought suicide (and other forms of violence) where these had been nearly unknown before. Here suicide reflects acculturation stress and difficult economic conditions. In other instances, the reservation had the effect of turning earlier aggressive patterns into self-aggression, namely suicide. Among the Apache, for example, the reservation system put an end to raiding and it controlled homicide, but aggression toward kinsmen and others could be expressed through suicide—"If you really want to hurt someone you kill yourself rather than him," that is, you leave him to deal with his remorse and the accusations of the community.

If in both these cases reservation life led to higher suicide rates, some Plains Indians showed lower rates. This was caused, however, by continuities rather than reversals in behavior patterns. Like the pre-reservation Crow Indian described by Clark Wissler, known as "Crazy-Dog-Wishing-to-Die," who has charged head-on into a Dakota raiding party, reservation Crow today sometimes follow a pattern of extreme risk-taking, for instance, driving a car into traffic in the wrong direction or walking into a freeway while drunk. In other words, "accidents" have been institutionalized substitutes for suicide. A different kind of continuity may be noted among the Navajo in the pattern of "revenge" suicide. The Navajo believe that all death not resulting from old age is unnatural, and that contact with violent death brings misfortune. Therefore, family strife may induce a person to suicide, planned so as to ensure that the body is found by a family member. Here the act is committed not to enable to individual to get out of an untenable situation but rather to stay in the situation in a more effective status, namely, to cause trouble as a ghost.

Since the cultural meanings attached to suicide are so variable, it is perhaps futile to seek generalizations that hold for all societies. Nevertheless, it is useful to make comparisons within limited geographical and cultural areas and to ask how the similarities and differences might reveal something of the social patterning of suicide. A volume of papers on suicide and homicide in eight African societies, presenting case material and analyses each by an anthropologist familiar with one of the eight tribes, offers a number of insights (1960). The volume editor, Paul Bohannan, observes that the rate of suicide in the eight societies is quite variable, although low, in general, in comparison with Europe. The most nearly universal feature of the African cases is the mode of suicide by hanging from trees. However, if one does not look only at rates but takes individual cases as diagnostic, some general points can be made about the social significance of suicide in Africa, which have resonances for our own society as well.

In the African cases, the act of suicide is almost always seen—both by the victim and the survivors—not as a destruction of the ego but as a means of achieving another form in which the new ego can act more effectively. The suicide may become a ghost who can bring harm to those who caused his troubles, or the act may be a way of forcing kin to take the victim's plight seriously or to carry out certain actions. While this perception of suicide as propelling a continuing effect rather than as self-obliteration may seem to apply only to cultures that believe in ghosts or in binding obligations of kinship, in fact it may also form part of the dynamics of suicide in our own society.

Another theme running through the African material is that suicide inevitably carries a quality of pollution. Typically, the tree on which a victim hanged himself will be cut down, because of its "contagion," and special provisions will be made for burial and mourning. The surviving kin are marked by an aura of pollution, which they can wipe out only by vengeance, rituals, or certain other acts. This pollution is familiar to our own culture, where even the most enlightened explanations of a suicide may prove inadequate to eradicate the enduring shame—or better, taint—surrounding the relatives.

Finally, a comparison of the patterning of suicide in the eight African societies allows us to inquire into the social etiology of suicide, to ask how suicide might be related to pressure points or structural tensions in a social system. That is, how do the requirements of life in different societies create contradictions for the individuals within them, leading to psychological stress and possibly to self-destructive action in given instances? Despite the variability among the eight societies and the small number of actual cases of suicide described, two kinds of causal patterns emerge: conflict in or inability to perform domestic roles, and failure in a status hierarchy.

Domestic-role conflict appears to account for many suicides of women among the Bunyoro or Uganda. In this society, women suffer the strains of polygamy and virilocality, the pattern whereby newly married couples take up residence in the village of the husband's kin. The problem usually stems not from jealousy among co-wives over the attentions of their husband, but rather from the public humiliation if a wife is neglected; the problem is compounded by the woman's separation from the support of her kinsmen and by the possible unwillingness of her brothers to retrieve her from a difficult domestic situation once the bride-price has been paid. (An interesting contrast to the Navajo situation, women in Bunyoro typically commit suicide away from the domestic compound, in the bush, symbolizing their feelings of separation from the husband's group). Domestic-role tensions account for suicide among African men as well, although less frequently than among women. A case from the Busoga of Uganda describes a quarrel between a village chief and his brother at a beer party. The brother shouts in a rage, "I will chop my bicycle to bits so you won't be able to inherit it." He runs off and tries to hang himself, but is prevented from doing so by his brothers; during the night, however, he succeeds. The strain in this situation comes from the fact that a father may name any son as his heir, usually leaving all his property to the single heir, but the choice is not made known until the father's death. The result is smoldering jealousies between brothers, which may escalate to unendurable proportions.

Suicide deriving from status-hierarchy strains affects men far more than women. A case in point is the Gisu of Uganda, where the peak incidence of suicide occurs among men between twenty-five and thirty-five. This age range comes after the period of initiation, which is marked by a solidarity among the young men going through circumcision ceremonies together. Once initiated, a man is separated from his age mates, and he marries. Now the inequality of rank with respect to his father becomes acute: the older man retains control of land and cattle, and prestige requires economic independence. Many men enter into migrant labor to try to improve their position at home, but on their return the conflict is often aggravated, since land is in short supply, and the authority of the father becomes more difficult to bear. Thus, the blockage of access to prestige, coupled with the absence of supportive social relationships, may trigger suicide among young adult men.

In more general terms, the African material suggests an underlying theme in the etiology of suicide: an inability to perform significant social roles, particularly when intensified to the point of social isolation. A poignant example is that of an old woman in Bunyoro, who found that she had a sickness that would require her to live in a special hut on the margins of the village, separated from her family and descendants. She committed suicide, not for fear of the illness but for fear of the isolation it would bring. There is surely a message in this for our own society.

REFERENCES

Benedict, R. *Patterns of culture*. New York: Mentor Books, 1934.

Bohannan, P. (Ed.) *African homicide and suicide*. Princeton: Princeton University Press, 1960.

Durkheim, E. *Suicide: A study in sociology* (English translation), London: Park Press, 1975. (See especially articles by Webb & Willard, Retterstol, Farber, Reynolds et al., Achte & Londquist, and IGA & Tatal).

Hendin, H. *Black suicide*. New York: Basic Books, 1969.

Malinowski, B. *Crime and custom in savage society*. London: Routledge & Kegan Paul, 1966, 1926.

Chapter 17

SELF-DESTRUCTIVE BEHAVIOR:
SLOW DYING

Samuel C. Klagsbrun

Of the many forms of slow deaths that professionals meet, certainly alcoholism and drug abuse stand out as major examples of slow suicide. One has to remember, however, that noncompliance with medical management also takes the form of slow suicide when looked at from a psychodynamic point of view as, for example, the juvenile diabetic who does not stick to a diet or who refuses to participate in the regular intake of insulin, the patient on the renal dialysis machine who abuses the diet regularly, the patient with pulmonary emphysema who continues to smoke. The issues involved in blatant continuing self-destructive behavior in the face of clear evidence of self-damage beg for attention. Certainly the problem of massive denial that is "I can overcome anything" plays a role in the personality of such patients. "I am above danger" reveals a grandiosity and a narcissism that is very hard to challenge in order to bring about help for the patient. Threatening the patient, warning the patient, using intellectual approaches is most frustrating in these clinical examples. What is required is a profound understanding and a therapeutic alliance with the patient along very traditional psychotherapeutic lines in order to get at the root of the self-destructive behavior. The odds are very much against successful intervention in this self-destructive pattern.

Slow dying must also be thought about by professionals as a worthy area of investigation in the field of chronic diseases. People who are paralyzed by virtue of accidents or strokes, people who have lingering diseases which will destroy their body slowly and their lives eventually, fall into a special category of concern for us. The attitude towards such patients has to be one of controlling and enhancing the quality of life that is available, and maximizing it realistically. For example, in an ascending paralysis the notion of staying ahead of each loss of motion by developing systems of pulleys, mechanical gadgets, and aids to anticipate limited motion and make up for it ahead of time by mechanical or electronic means will invite the patient to maintain mastery and to develop an attitude of control on the face of what is otherwise a horrible anticipated future. The treatment of those patients must be based on reality mixed in with a tremendous amount of practical support. The key factor here is practical management. Professionals must come in with attempted solutions offered rather than simply with empty words of support.

The diagnostic considerations involved in this field include most certainly the question of a sense of sadness and loss in the face of understandable and recognizable loss of function versus an exaggerated reaction, a depression which goes beyond sadness and mourning for loss in the face of loss of function. This distinction is sometimes hard to make and requires knowing a patient quite well. Working with a family or knowledgeable other people is a helpful and important asset in determining the answer to the question, "Is it depression or is it sadness?"

The drain on a staff working with these populations is enormous. In order to maintain continuity of care by not having a high rotation out of a service or out of the field staff support must be built into any system tackling these clinical issues. The support must be built in during the course of the working day rather than simply crisis intervention when the staff has had it. To respond on a crisis level alone is to respond too late.

Entering into this field requires the professional to anticipate having to face basic questions of morality, ethics, and religion. For example, a patient who develops an important relationship with a professional and who is facing slow death may wish at some point to ask the professional to participate in their death by hastening it because the quality of life has become intolerable. A patient with myasthenia gravis may ask a therapist to help them die because the amount of loss of control is no longer tolerable. Therapists working in this field therefore must come to terms with questions of euthanasia and decide for themselves what they would be comfortable in discussing, or as the case may be, staying away from when working with this patient population. Clarifying one's own values is a prerequisite for entering this most difficult area of treatment.

INDEX